1008116962

The Next Step

The Next Step

Today's Methods for Today's Math

Edited by
James Freemyer

ROWMAN & LITTLEFIELD
Lanham • Boulder • New York • London

Published by Rowman & Littlefield
An imprint of The Rowman & Littlefield Publishing Group, Inc.
4501 Forbes Boulevard, Suite 200, Lanham, Maryland 20706
www.rowman.com

6 Tinworth Street, London SE11 5AL, United Kingdom

British Library Cataloguing in Publication Information Available

Library of Congress Cataloging-in-Publication Data Available

ISBN: 978-1-4758-4445-0 (cloth)
ISBN: 978-1-4758-4446-7 (electronic)
ISBN: 978-1-4758-4447-4 (pbk)

Contents

Preface

This book is dedicated to America's mathematics teachers, who have been asked to teach more conceptually while simultaneously motivating more students of all ability levels to willingly embrace further upper-level mathematics content and courses. This is a BIG ASK! Math teachers are being expected to overhaul their teaching approach as principals expect more extensive work and reflection than what was required of new teachers first learning the profession. Can teachers be expected to embrace this crusade alone, isolated in a classroom, charged to go *back* to the effort of earlier days while being left alone to design and implement *the future*?

If Vygotsky is correct, as cited by Smith and Stein (2011), that "Research tells us that complex knowledge and skills are learned through social interaction" (p. 1), then students require extensive interaction in the classroom. This fact alone demands major classroom structure adaptations and is now expected of all mathematics teachers. We recognize the need for student social interaction due to this request for student complexity, but we often miss recognizing the exact same need for teacher complexity in designing such lessons.

To accommodate this, mathematics teachers are being asked not only to adjust their teaching approach, but in essence to overhaul it. To succeed, teachers too must be provided with the same opportunities for consistent collaboration through social interaction that such major adaptations demand. Principals must lead the way. They must provide the opportunities and resources necessary for a successful process of change.

After reading this book, a principal will comprehend the enormity of the task each mathematics teacher faces. School leaders will be able to design a growth plan based on a plethora of approaches. Mathematics teachers will experience the assistance they have desperately needed.

Acknowledgments

Principals and teachers in Indiana, California, Ireland, Great Britain, South Korea, and Japan welcomed me into their classrooms and set aside time for interviews, allowing me to experience firsthand how teacher collaboration and principal support could provide opportunities for the professional growth and development of mathematics teachers around the world. Special thanks to colleagues Dr. John O'Donoghue, Dr. Olivia Fitzmaurice, and Dr. Patrick Johnson from Limerick University in Ireland for supporting my research while I was there on a Fulbright Scholarship. Thanks to each coauthor who responded to my call and invested heavily into the project. Many thanks to the graphic artist, Nathan Freemyer, for powerful illustrations and diagrams. Finally, to my wife, who provided editing assistance and moral support, I appreciate you so much.

Introduction

This work is a result of four years of research in the United States, Europe, and Asia, examining how principals were working together with local mathematics teachers to explore ways to engage and motivate a growing number of mathematics students to consider exploring the possibility of a STEM career. Teachers often struggle to adapt to the changing pedagogical approaches required of mathematics teachers. Engaging all students, not just those of high ability, in the conversation surrounding the complexities of mathematics, is a challenge that teachers around the world share.

This research demonstrated that, when teachers were able to collaborate with their colleagues, they were able to make significant progress in overhauling their approach to teaching mathematics. Returning to the process of learning how to teach from a different perspective, while engaging more students in shared learning by expanding student dialogue through teacher interaction is reminiscent of first learning to teach. To expect teachers to back up and start over is a big ask. Doing it in isolation, apart from dialogue and assistance from colleagues, is simply not feasible.

Yet many schools mandate that mathematics teachers improve without meaningful research-based support. Schools in Europe and Asia, that realize the enormity of the called-for task and provide help in the form of release time for peer collaborative planning, observation, and research, experience major advances in student mind-sets regarding the subject of mathematics. Teaching changes that engage all students in productive struggle and social dialogue reaped a cultural shift in student attitude, in addition to overall growth in academic achievement.

The first three chapters provide mathematics teachers and school leaders with the rationale for major changes in the pedagogical approach to teaching middle and high school mathematics. Chapters 4–6 provide the reader with research-based ideas for transforming mathematics classrooms. Chapter 7 provides school leaders with a theoretical approach, to design and implement a local school change initiative.

Chapter 8 provides teachers and leaders with resources for adapting the way math is taught. Chapter 9 provides examples of how very effective schools in Europe and Asia have handled the transition to a more conceptual, student-centered teaching approach. Chapter 10 makes the case for the importance of improved student/teacher relationships as students are engaged in productive struggle and conceptual understanding. Chapter 11 is a vignette that emphasizes the impact that a different mathematics approach would make on our youth.

Chapter One

The Call to Change

James Freemyer

PRE-READING REFLECTION

1. Why are world leaders calling for mathematics teachers around the globe to make dramatic changes in the way they teach their content?
2. Why have so many countries, including the United States, struggled to motivate more students to explore careers in science, technology, engineering, and mathematics (STEM)?
3. How can local school leaders encourage our best teachers and assist others to engage more students in the study of the upper levels of mathematics? What role should school leadership play?
4. How are successful countries like the United States, Ireland, Great Britain, South Korea, and Japan at helping local teachers focus on the conceptual understanding of mathematics?

WHAT TO EXPECT IN THIS CHAPTER

What is wrong with the teaching of mathematics in the United States? The majority of our schools have adequate facilities and ample time to teach the material. Our teachers are professionals who are devoted to helping young people learn and grow. Yet most mathematicians would agree that the way we teach mathematics must change if we expect a greater percentage of young people to choose careers in the STEM areas (Guerrero, 2014; Lubienski, 2011).

Some of our greatest thinkers in mathematics education have a plan to address the goal of increasing the number of students who succeed at high levels. They advocate teaching that involves sense making with a more conceptual approach while unapologetically challenging students with increased cognitive demand using practical mathematics problems (Boaler, 2009; James and Pollard, 2011; Schoenfeld, 2015; Usiskin, 2015).

Why do the majority of mathematics teachers find it difficult to transition to this approach? What lessons can be learned from some of our more effective mathematics teachers? Should teachers focus on certain particulars as they transition to a more cognitive teaching approach? What assistance to our teachers is needed before effective change can occur?

THE CALL TO CHANGE:
MORE STEM STUDENTS NEEDED

Teachers in the STEM arena face unprecedented and overwhelming expectations of change as educators around the world strive to better prepare secondary students for the rigors associated with STEM courses. According to Matt Larson (2016), former president of the National Council of Teachers of Mathematics (NCTM), "Today, it seems as if nearly everyone agrees that high school mathematics needs to change. For far too long high school mathematics has not worked for far too many students" (2016, p. 1).

Clearly we need a new approach to better motivate more students to take advanced mathematics courses. The consensus solution is to provide more thought-provoking, conceptually based challenges designed to help students of all ability levels comprehend difficult ideas. This approach almost seems counterproductive, that one could motivate more students to engage in mathematics by requiring more in-depth, challenging content. Teachers worldwide have increased their focus on helping students experience shared learning through increased student-initiated dialogue focused on sustained think time.

Educators concur that collaboration is a real key to helping students reflect on difficult concepts. Yet school leaders fail to acknowledge that teachers face the exact same challenges as their students when teachers envision how to shift their paradigm of effective pedagogy from telling students through a procedural approach to requiring more of a contemplative, discovery approach. Should teachers, who have been asked to make such extensive changes in their teaching approach, be denied of the same collaborative assistance? Do we recognize that students need the benefit of working in groups but expect teachers to go it alone?

A national survey in Ireland in 2014 conducted as a result of a Fulbright Scholarship confirmed that faculty development alone does not generate significant change in a teaching approach (Freemyer, Johnson, Fitzmaurice, 2016). After three years of intensive faculty development for 100 percent of the nation's mathematics teachers, more than 91 percent said the old approach was just as effective. A national survey (n = 147) indicated that Irish mathematics teachers agree with the new conceptual approach but they are not convinced that the old procedural approach is less effective. After a national commitment to retrain every math teacher using a three-year process, not much changed. See table 1.1, which follows.

If students require more focused dialogue to spur sustained change, then the same must be true for teachers. Faculty development alone is simply not enough to spark real change, especially if initiated at the national level. What is being asked of our teachers is much more than teaching a new curriculum. Teacher collaboration is critical to improving teaching approaches. Why not concede that pedagogical growth is tied to teacher collaboration? Why not replace destination learning with pilgrimage discovery for both students and teachers alike?

Global competition has all but mandated real-life approaches to STEM education, yet academic leaders have grossly lagged in assisting teachers with the paradigm shift. Preparing students for national and

Table 1.1. How effective do you believe a more traditional approach to the teaching of mathematics (which includes more teacher modeling and student direct practice) is in preparing students for Junior Certificate and Leaving Certificate examinations?

		Frequency	Percent	Valid Percent	Cumulative Percent
Valid	Totally Effective	13	8.8	8.8	8.8
	Mostly Effective	66	44.9	44.9	53.7
	Somewhat Effective	55	37.4	37.4	91.2
	Nice but Not Necessary	3	2.0	2.0	93.2
	Somewhat Ineffective	7	4.8	4.8	98.0
	Mostly Ineffective	3	2.0	2.0	100.0
	Total	147	100.0	100.0	

Source: Freemyer, Johnson, and Fitzmaurice, 2016.

international markets of the twenty-first century requires equipping them with the skill sets necessary for success. In the STEM arena, mathematics teachers must have help, encouragement, and guidance as they employ these new conceptual approaches. Is a fifty-minute daily planning period sufficient for teachers to change their paradigm, develop new conceptual approaches, assess student understanding more frequently, adjust their approach, and spend more time successfully helping all ability levels of students?

Global competition and the need for a more high-tech workforce have left nations around the world scrambling to better prepare young people to compete for these jobs. One key component of the United States' plan introduced in 2013 was the need to improve P–12 STEM instruction. The Department of Education was directed by President Obama to "support partnerships among school districts and universities . . . to transform teaching and learning" (5-Year Strategic Plan, page ii). The need for U.S. math teachers to be more effective is indicated by the disparity between the numbers of U.S. students who earn STEM degrees and students in other countries (Stearns, Morgan, Capraro, and Capraro, 2012).

The Department of Education was quick to realize that teachers must have university professors and effective colleagues as collaborative partners if we expect real growth within the rank and file of our mathematics teachers. Transforming teaching and learning is a big ask. Simply providing faculty development and then mandating change has proven throughout history to be wholly inadequate. Recognizing the enormity of the expected change is the first real step for reform. Providing collaborative planning, joint observation, and significant discourse is essential if real growth is to be expected. Exemplary schools in Europe and Asia have documented this fulfillment of need and validated this approach.

Preparing students for the national and international markets of the future requires equipping a greater percentage of them with the necessary skill sets for success. High school mathematics scores, as measured by international tests, have remained flat for more than a decade and been sliding relative to our international peers (Larson, 2017). To examine ways to address these issues, this research began by going directly to our better teachers and asking them the secrets of their success. The research presented in this book summarizes what was learned from these highly effective teachers from Indiana, Ireland, and the U.K. Research conclusions from mathematics teachers from Japan and South Korea will be included in chapter 9.

Most mathematics researchers would agree that the way we teach mathematics must change if we expect a greater percentage of young people to choose careers in the STEM areas (Boaler, 2009; Boston, Dillon, Smith, and Miller, 2017; Darling-Hammond and Bransford, 2005; Devine, Fahie, and Mcgillicuddy, 2013; Freemyer, Fitzmaurice, and Johnson, 2015; Guerrero, 2014; Hattie, 2012; Lubienski, 2011; Schoenfeld, 2011, Smith and Stein, 2011; Usiskin, 2015). The consensus of researchers is that teachers must employ a more conceptual approach.

For far too long conceptual understanding has taken a back seat to procedural understanding in mathematics classrooms. As far back as 2001, Smith characterized the changes as more "transformative than additive" (2011, p. 3). Conceptual learning, as defined by John Hattie (2012) is paramount—"teachers see learning occurring or not occurring, they intervene in calculated and meaningful ways to alter the direction of the learning . . . and provide students with multiple opportunities and alternatives for developing strategies based on surface and deep levels of learning some content or domain matter, leading to students building conceptual understanding" (p. 18).

In early high school courses, the brighter students catch on easily, but they are infrequently challenged with more in-depth problems. The end result is that, when material becomes more challenging in precalculus and calculus, students assume the resulting struggles indicate they should not continue taking math courses, so they pursue other interests. Had they learned to work through more challenging, conceptual material earlier, students would come to appreciate the challenges and fulfillment that deeper understanding brings. More students are likely to continue in the STEM area if they experience more rewarding productive struggle earlier.

Average and below-average students also benefit from a more conceptual teaching approach. They learn that struggle is good within an atmosphere of psychological safety. They can learn to better appreciate that mistakes inform learning and that collaboration provides avenues for growth. A conceptual underpinning allows more students to tackle additional advanced ideas in later courses. Success with difficult problems smooths the road to higher learning. Yet most teachers are being asked to attempt these new conceptual teaching approaches by spending more time planning, assessing effectiveness, and adjusting lessons while teaching, all in a busy teacher's spare time. We simply cannot expect significant change without local level help.

Both procedural and conceptual approaches are important in effective mathematics classrooms. This research opted to go directly to the source for possible changes and seek ideas directly from some of our best teachers in the field. Observing and interviewing effective teachers in five countries affirmed that some teachers know how to motivate more students to reach higher levels of mathematics understanding. The research affirmed that what is needed is to engage more students in productive struggle throughout most mathematics lessons.

Focusing energy on the best and brightest students is no longer an effective teaching strategy. Our best teachers understand this. Targeting more students of all ability levels to choose STEM careers is critical. NCTM reinforces the need to impact all students and equally assist them to reach high levels of understanding. We are not satisfied with impacting just our brightest students. We also should not be satisfied influencing just the brightest mathematics teachers. Being satisfied with a few good mathematics teachers within a school is no longer enough.

THE WAY TO CHANGE: A LOCAL FOCUS

For some time our approach to change has been a national mandate handed down to stakeholders at the local level. Yet our record of engendering real change has been anemic through the years. Not only was the national focus of the "new math" initiative of the middle of the twentieth century a failure, it spawned a backlash response called "back-to-the-basics."

The current focus on the Common Core has found politicians defending more traditional approaches while parents and students are often frustrated. It is time for a real change! The academic world agrees on the need to change. We just need a system that can effectively help our dedicated mathematics teachers carry out the long-standing call for change. The research provides academic leaders at the school level with ideas for moving mathematics teachers from "pockets of excellence to a system of excellence" (Principles to Action, Executive Summary 2014, p. 2).

According to two change experts, J. Steward Black and Hal Gregersen (2008), effective change must transpire at the local level, not at the national or organizational level. They affirm that *It Starts with*

One, which is the title of their popular book. Focus on the local level in this context means that principals must be tasked to lead the way to changes in the culture, one mathematics teacher at a time. Emphasis on the group, with a focus on each individual teacher's journey for change, provides hope for improved student scores and subsequent interest. The principal is uniquely positioned to lead the change, support the change, encourage small steps, and reward teachers for reaching more and more students.

The goal is not just to reach students but to inspire more and more of them to pursue advanced studies in the STEM arena. Teachers need assistance. The goal is nothing short of generating a substantial new cultural experience for all students. The new culture is the antithesis of what is currently found in many of our mathematics classrooms, where teachers portray that mathematics is hard, disjointed, and boring, and that only the best students can succeed. Teachers must grapple with new ideas and alternative teaching approaches.

Teachers must experiment with new methodologies. They must come to grips with the concept that the old right approach is now the new wrong approach to the teaching of mathematics, as Black and Gregersen (2008) would say it. Mathematics teachers need principals' support, allowing more planning time and more collaboration opportunities as we adjust to new approaches. High school principals can make a real difference in encouraging mathematics teachers in their quest to inspire more students. First we must examine what our best teachers can tell us about successfully making the needed changes.

MORE THAN A FEW GOOD TEACHERS

Many schools are satisfied with a few good mathematics teachers. Yet every student deserves an outstanding teacher. Academic leaders have been slow to engage in the dialogue about academic reform, for mathematics teachers in particular. Matt Larson called for additional support for professional learning by mathematics teachers (Larson 2017) and Darling-Hammond (2006) stressed the importance of teachers becoming "adaptive experts" (p. 3) as they learn and grow. In addition, research conducted by Sanders and Rivers (1996) indicated that student math achievement was negatively impacted by ineffective mathematics teachers.

One Indiana teacher interviewed for this research was able to spend one year at a special assignment where he assisted mathematics teachers across the country in their preparation for successfully teaching Advanced Placement (AP) courses. Teaching more conceptually is a challenge often theoretically embraced by our AP teaching faculty. From his travels he estimated that only 7 percent of mathematics teachers actually excel at their role. He estimated that 60 percent of mathematics teachers are average, with 33 percent being poor at their job (Freemyer, 2016). According to Stigler and Hiebert (2009), authors of *The Teaching Gap*, "the United States has no system for improving our teaching. We are always reforming but not always improving" (p. xviii).

Now, more than ever, mathematics teachers must improve in their work. The goal is clear. U.S. teachers must inspire more high school students to choose careers in STEM areas. The path to success also is clear. We must better prepare math teachers to inspire and equip the next generation of young people in STEM subjects. The specifics for accomplishing these goals, however, continue to elude us. How do high school principals guide math teachers to raise scores and inspire young people to consider careers in STEM areas?

A large part of assessing our success in this endeavor must include tracking the number of students who continue to take advanced courses in the STEM arena. If principals assessed mathematics teachers' effectiveness in part by documenting the number of students who continue to take advanced courses, the teaching approach would change radically. Why not begin now?

This focus involves changing the classroom culture by transforming each student's experience to a positive, encouraging encounter directed at exciting further study. Ironically the correct path forward has obtained widespread acceptance in developed countries around the world. The unrecognized, elusive component that constitutes best practices in the teaching of mathematics and which will promote such a culture remains confined to some of this country's best teachers. This must change.

PATH TO EFFECTIVE CHANGE

If we know what should be done, why not just do it? That is a good question. Knowing what should be done to combat cancer and finding ways to do that effectively are two very different things. Understanding what should be done is always just the first step. There are two major approaches that usually follow the identification of a need: a top-down approach to mandated change or a collaborative approach accenting a joint effort from the bottom up. According to Stigler and Hiebert (2009), "The American approach has been to write and distribute reform documents and ask teachers to implement the recommendations contained in such documents" (p. 2). The level of the transformation requires a more effective change approach.

Nothing less than a major cultural shift is needed. We must reject the paradigm that mathematics courses are hard, disconnected, and boring and change to expectations of mathematics courses that are challenging, intriguing, and very rewarding. This would require what John Hattie (2012) described as teachers with a clear passion who "challenge . . . intellectual and imaginative capacities way out to horizons unsullied by self-fulfilling minimalist expectations" (p. ix). Hattie (2012) suggested that effective teachers must be nurturing and caring with humanity and sensitivity having "genuine respect, enlightened discipline, and imaginative flair," (p. ix). Hattie advocates maximizing student potential for advanced schooling by inspiring a love of learning.

A recent case study chronicles an approach directed at helping leaders during these turbulent times: (a) evaluating current teaching approaches; (b) creating faculty development sessions aimed at increasing student rigor, academic engagement, and continuous in-classroom assessment coupled with real-life applications; (c) establishing a collaborative teaching approach to ongoing experimentation and improvement; (d) addressing leadership issues vital to successfully achieving significant organizational change; and (e) collaboration with science departments and other fields (Freemyer, Johnson, and Fitzmaurice, 2017).

THEORETICAL FRAMEWORK FOR EFFECTIVE MATHEMATICS TEACHING

The framework for this study was developed by Alan Schoenfeld: "Teaching for Robust Understanding" or the TRU Framework (Schoenfeld 2016). The framework is designed to focus classroom attention on components that matter most in a mathematics classroom. There are other such frameworks that could serve as well, including NCTM's *Principles to Action*. This framework was used for research that began in 2014. It includes "five dimensions of classroom activity designed to produce students who are powerful thinkers" (TRU website: http://map.mathshell.org/trumath.php). The five dimensions include the following headings with practices identified by the sixty-three original mathematics teachers interviewed, identified, and confirmed by 154 teachers in Ireland.

Dr. Alan Schoenfeld confirmed alignment of the twenty-eight components derived from research in the United States and Europe to his five-dimension framework in a personal communication of May 30, 2016. The research outcomes generated from Indiana, Ireland, and U.K. teachers were tabulated within this theoretical framework.

I. The Mathematics—Understanding content pedagogy, creating connections to previous learning, understanding where students will struggle.
II. Cognitive Demand—Creating an environment where students engage in productive struggle, create their own sense, and work to understand concepts in mathematics.
III. Access to Mathematical Content—All students engaged in learning throughout the lesson not just the best and brightest.
IV. Agency, Authority, and Identity—Students see themselves as able to do mathematics and take pride in their accomplishments. They are mathematicians!
V. Use of Assessment—Students are involved in formative assessment throughout a lesson in such a way that the teacher can determine how much the students understand and how to guide them further.

This framework serves as the theoretical perspective by which middle and high school teachers can structure their approaches to improved instruction. This book will guide school leaders (department chairs, assistant principals, and principals) through this framework to provide a clear focus for mathematics teachers' revised approach that is geared to helping a vast majority of students to consider advanced study in the STEM arena. Research conducted in Indiana, Ireland, the U.K. affirm this approach (Freemyer, Johnson, and Fitzmaurice, 2017). Subsequent research in South Korea and Japan, as shared at the National Council of Teachers of Mathematics conference in 2018 in Washington, D.C., extends the research to Asia (Freemyer, 2018).

RESEARCH IMPLICATION:
REACHING ALL STUDENTS

Teachers understand the importance of the need for change. We simply must motivate a much larger percentage of students to continue to pursue advanced courses in the STEM arena. Well-paying jobs will be waiting for those students who accomplish this goal. According to Smith and Stein (2011), "Our country needs highly trained workers who can wrestle with complex problems. Gone are the days when basic skills could be counted on to yield high paying jobs and acceptable standards of living" (p.1). But can more than our best and brightest students succeed in understanding the more abstract concepts that comprise much of the advanced levels in these fields?

Carol Dweck's research provides encouraging research results for this discussion. Her research underscores the viability of the substantial change in our approach to teaching math. Her concept regarding the importance of a growth mind-set rather than a fixed mind-set provides a blueprint to help mathematics teachers teach more conceptually, orchestrating more productive dialogue advocated by Smith and Stein (2011) in their illuminating book, *5 Practices for Orchestrating Productive Mathematics Discussions*. Applying her approach to the need for a more conceptual approach to teaching would result in targeting all students with productive struggle, asking them to grapple with big ideas that lead to more conceptual understanding.

Instead of worrying about a grade and assessment (a fixed mind-set), students would focus on the process, effort, strategies, focus, perseverance, and improvement according to Carol Dweck's TED Talk. The daily outcome becomes yet or not yet, instead of pass or fail. Students would grow to love the challenging process rather than simply seek the right or wrong outcomes. Students would learn to be less worried about "am I right or wrong" and more focused on "sticking to it, even (especially) when it's not going well" (Dweck, 2016, p. 7). A growth mind-set undergirds an approach that focuses on grappling with changing concepts.

A growth mind-set makes it acceptable for students of different ability levels to work within the same classroom that is focused on a more conceptual understanding of mathematics. Like walking up the stairs that lead to the goal of conceptual understanding, the brighter students take fewer yet larger steps while average students must take more numerous and smaller steps. Below-average students climb the path to conceptual understanding by taking even more small steps, but all eventually need to reach the same required level. Mathematics teachers are charged with coordinating and orchestrating each student's learning every day.

Through the process of comprehending conceptual mathematics principles, both average and below-average students often make more mistakes when voicing their thought processes. Carol Dweck's approach emphasizes that such minor missteps are just part of the journey to significant conceptual understanding. Wrong ideas should be dissected for pockets of validity through small-group and whole-class dialogue, and analyzed to spawn more conceptual understanding. These errors in thinking become smaller steps that ultimately take the individual and the class to clearer understanding; they are not indications of overall capability. Japanese classrooms observed in Chicago and in Tokyo highlight this academic approach (Freemyer, 2018).

Within this framework, mistakes are considered to be an important part of the process and actually by the means which students move the ball of understanding forward. Like a soccer team headed toward the goal, imperfect passes can still be very effective. When confronting opposition challenges, players adjust and proceed toward the goal. A positive class climate accommodates and can feed on wrong thinking without negative feeling toward students who advance slower. Students should never hesitate to answer for fear of being wrong. Positive reinforcement encourages rather than stifles productive struggle. Classes that value insightful attempts over correctness spawn in-depth learning.

Figure 1.1. Teacher helping three students up set of stairs. *Credit:* Nathan Freemyer, graphic artist

According to Vygotsky as cited by Smith and Stein (2011), "Research tells us that complex knowledge and skills are learned through social interaction" (p. 1). Carol Dweck's approach provides a framework to understand how mathematics teachers can inspire more and more students to consider the substantial benefits of taking more advanced courses in the STEM area. The rewards for doing well in the STEM arena can be significant. Teachers in Ireland are coached to emphasize to students that success in STEM areas is worth the challenge and will most likely lead to a better life.

Our most effective mathematics teachers in Indiana, Ireland, and the U.K. have underscored this importance. Professor Paul Conway of the University of Limerick and former President of the Educational Studies Association of Ireland (ESAI) posited in a personal interview that mathematics teachers need local support, resources, and ideas, including networking with peers and mentors in order to create impactful improvement in student learning (personal communication, November 12, 2014). He surmised that the better teachers in the United States are utilizing these effective approaches; now they need to spread the approaches to more and more teachers.

According to Stigler and Hiebert (2009), "compared with other countries, the United States clearly lacks a system for developing professional knowledge and for giving the teachers the opportunity to learn about teaching" (p. 13). What we learned from our best teachers was that improving mathematics instruction included an increase in academic rigor through real-life, problem-based approaches. This approach, which involves a more conceptual understanding of critical mathematics content, must be focused on students of all abilities. Researchers like Carol Dweck (2016) hypothesized that a growth mind-set enables teachers and leaders to target students of all ability levels in motivating more and more students to continue advanced courses.

Using this same logic, can mathematics teachers be expected to just attend faculty development sessions and then change their entire teaching approach? If Vygotsky is correct and complex knowledge and skills are learned through social interaction, should principals not provide collaborative opportunities for our mathematics teachers? Principals must do their part in designing an approach that promotes collaboration. Does it always just come down to a money issue? Can we afford not to invest in our mathematics teachers? The future awaits the answer.

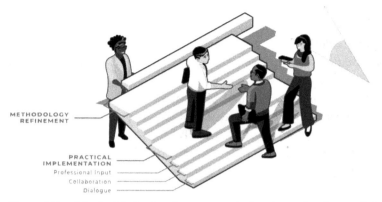

METHODOLOGY
REFINEMENT

PRACTICAL
IMPLEMENTATION
Professional Input
Collaboration
Dialogue

Figure 1.2. Principal helps teachers up a set of stairs as teachers collaborate and help each other. *Credit:* Nathan Freemyer, graphic artist

SUMMARY

The call to change is unmistakable. Nations around the world are scrambling to retrain mathematics teachers in ways that encourage conceptual understanding with the hope that more students will take STEM-type courses at the higher levels. Ireland's leaders are so convinced that this is the approach of the future that they have mandated that every mathematics teacher in the nation be retrained to teach more conceptually in a continuing process or in an ongoing process. In an effort to better prepare their youth with this more conceptual approach, they have realigned their national curriculum, revamped their high-stakes testing, and provided extra incentives in college entrance scores for students who do well in mathematics.

Yet mathematics teachers have not fully embraced these new approaches. When asked in my national survey of mathematics teachers in Ireland, more than 91 percent of teachers admitted they still believed that their old, procedural approach (back to the basics), which they learned as they moved through the curriculum was adequate. Changing ingrained teaching approaches will not be easy. According to Senge, "the approach of surfacing, testing, and internal pictures of how the world works" (Senge 1990, p. 174) helps provide a time-tested approach to effective change. What is holding us back?

Chapter Two

The Case for Professional Learning Communities

Keith Walters

PRE-READING REFLECTION

1. How are adults' and children's developmental responses to change similar? Different?
2. How does your typical pattern of response to change impact your acceptance, adoption, and implementation of educational reform?
3. What are the distinctions between memorization/repetition and problem-solving/inquiry pedagogies?
4. What are some of your positive and negative experiences with professional learning communities?

WHAT TO EXPECT IN THIS CHAPTER

Daily classroom challenges are rarely neutral. Observing students celebrating the joy of successful academic achievement inspires teachers to energetically embrace the profession. Moving a student from the proclamation "Math is stupid" through "I can't believe I just got this problem right" to "I am effectively using geometric formulas to design a dress for the school play" confirms a teacher's belief that education can change lives. Conversely, student apathy, low test scores, and explicit behavioral rebellion initiate fissures within the teacher's professional self-concept.

CHANGE IS HARD

Occupational frustration intensifies as the teacher seeks to navigate cyclical governmental reforms. One point in the tessellation is the authentic learning emphasis, which includes Dewey's Laboratory school (1902), project-based curriculum (1970s), integrated curriculum (1990s), and Common Core (2015). A second point is the foundational knowledge emphasis, which consists of the Elementary and Secondary Education Act (1965), the Back to Basics Movement (1984), and No Child Left Behind (2001).

The pendulum perception hints at a disconnect between student learning needs and political maneuvers initiated for election success. The result can be an educator narrative that asserts "this new reform will soon pass. Avoid the authorities. Keep doing what you have always done, and nobody will get hurt." Sadly, the passive-aggressive response is often transferred to district and site initiatives, such as collaborative math lesson studies.

An anti-change, status-quo temperament is hidden within the words of the veteran teacher. Three themes often emerge as potential driving forces for the resistant disposition. The macro-level explanation focuses on the subconscious, cultural influences of U.S. individualism. Characteristics include justifying decisions based on one's own preferences, modifying behaviors in an effort to minimize negative consequences, and establishing amicable communities through the systematic obstruction of contrarian views. Successful implementation reinforces the perception that egocentric views of truth are solely sufficient to guide and direct all life decisions (Kraft, 2009).

The mezzo-level description draws attention to the teacher's cognitive script. The main premise highlights an individual's tendency to use the skills learned during past successes to navigate current challenges. Classroom application starts with the teacher's decision to implement lesson plan activities that mirror the strategies the teacher found beneficial when they were a student. The process continues with the teacher subconsciously fixating on current students who leverage the strategy on their path to academic success. Belief in the tried-and-true pedagogy is now reinforced, making the need for change irrelevant (Darling-Hammond, 2006, 2010).

The micro-level explanation assesses the impact of emotions. Goleman (2005) classified emotions into two levels. Conscious emotion encompasses the ability to recognize and control feelings. Unconscious emotions are unidentified and unmanageable. Positive unconscious emotions often create a sense of serenity. Negative unconscious emotions can push a teacher into a downward spiral. The progression starts with a failure to recognize key environmental context clues, causing the teacher to miss necessary lesson plan adjustment and distort assessment of actual student learning. Self-preservation inclinations then propel the teacher to seek the emotional safety typically found in reengaging tried-and-true routines and behaviors.

Common to the macro-, mezzo-, and micro-level rationales is a nurture-based perspective of development. Palmer (1998) noted that many contemporary educators were educated in a system that supports the adoption of hierarchical principles. Knowledge is absolute. Teacher expertise guarantees mistake-free transfer of information. Efficient memorization skills as well as the production of right responses mark student success. The problem, Parker argued, is the systematic destruction of critical, creative thinking. In a world where the availability of information continues to exponentially grow, dynamic learning opportunities where truth, remains but paths to discovery are varied must now replace scripted, linear lessons.

Palmer (2000) acknowledged the difficulty of dispositional change. Issuing mandates will be ineffective. Providing autonomy will offer minimal transformation. The reason, Palmer suggested, is one's approach to teaching. Those adopting the occupational approach will exploit compliance in exchange for career ladder advancement. Those seeking a vocation perspective will welcome dreams of unlimited possibility.

Palmer (2000) defined vocation as a progression that starts when one is willing to honestly contemplate the impact of personal failure. Focus is on holistic reflection. Assumptions of perfection are rejected. The next step is identifying and addressing barriers that are preventing corrective actions. This mind-set of humility serves as the beginning of a new pilgrimage. The destination is discernable. The path is perceptible. Modifications to the initial direction one takes is expected. The definition of success moves from reaching a specific point to maintaining faithfulness to the journey.

Vignette

Dr. Martinez has never been more excited for the first month of school. As a recent doctorate in Educational Leadership graduate, Dr. Martinez's belief in the societal transformation potential of schools is at an all-time high. Even more exhilarating is her recent promotion to principal of Rosa Park High School.

Situated in an industrial section of a large metropolitan city, Rosa Park High School draws from lower-middle-class neighborhoods. Student achievement has been stagnant, with math achievement test scores being the lowest. Parents and students seem ambivalent. Area business managers, however, are becoming increasingly frustrated as graduates no longer possess the basic skills necessary to be successful employees.

Prior to the start of the academic year, the superintendent informed Dr. Martinez that she was expected to immediately raise test scores. This did not appear to be impossible. Key to her plan was the school's well-established professional learning communities. Agendas and minutes of the last academic year highlighted a systematic approach to reviewing math test score data. An unsolicited invitation to the first meeting further encouraged her optimism.

Dr. Martinez was a few minutes late for the meeting. Mr. Jones, the department chair, was talking: "Since this is the beginning of the year, let's start our review with our state's common core standards' category titled 'making sense of problems and persevering in solving them.'"

Ms. VandenBerg, a twenty-year veteran, spontaneously erupted, "The reading level of our students has become so bad that most of them cannot even read simple word problems. How do you expect us to teach students who cannot read?"

Without missing a beat, Mr. Cooper added, "What's worse is that the students in the remedial classes cannot even add and subtract."

One comment after another emphasized student deficiencies. Hesitantly, Dr. Martinez entered into the conversation. "I can appreciate the difficulty you are experiencing as you work with students who are below grade level. Yet we have an obligation to move each child toward higher levels of achievement. Does anyone have any ideas?"

The group sat quiet for a moment. Mr. Jones was the first to speak. "Last year, in the remedial class, we had a weekly timed arithmetic test. This helped us improve our annual standardized test scores. Should we do this again?"

"Yes," Ms. VandenBerg proclaimed.

"And, why don't we add a timed story problem section to the test?" Mr. Cooper added.

The conversations continued. Dr. Martinez noticed that each participant emphasized the importance of adopting memorization and repetition pedagogy. Most disconcerting to Dr. Martinez was the growing enthusiasm the conversations were generating. How was she going to help this group of teachers understand and embrace the need for change?

LOOKING INTO THE MIRROR:
THE TEACHER AS AN INDIVIDUAL

Instinctual Responses to Reform

Dr. Martinez's belief in the principles of holistic development impacts the decisions she will make as she systematically works to nurture the school culture. A holistic developmental view stresses the integrated relationships among individual, social, emotional, cognitive, and spiritual growth. Simplistically summarized, an individual's past creates a cognitive script that is used to interpret the present and make decisions for the future.

The vibrant, interactive relationship between an individual's cognitive script and environmental stimuli impacts new learning. Sousa (2017) postulated that the overwhelming quantities of stimuli bombarding a person's five senses is beyond the brain's processing capabilities. The need for expediency prioritizes physical or emotional risk stimuli. Safety coupled with interest and curiosity direct new learning concentration. Maturation refines the individual's interpretations of safety, interest, and curiosity. The potential outcome is a negative correlation between aging and willingness to change.

Synthesizing safety, interest, and curiosity with essentialist U.S. educational practices proffers insights into a teacher's status-quo acquiescence. Personal, positive encounters with traditional occupational content knowledge, patriotic citizenship, and self-sacrificing or common good curricula often evoke passion for better pedagogical implementation rather than change. In addition, acknowledging the U.S. economy's need for trained and untrained workers can sustain differentiated practices such as Resource Room, General Education, GATE, and Advanced Placement classes.

Teachers supportive of diverse student learning outcomes will envision little need for educational reform. Darling-Hammond (2006, 2010) noted four areas where a lack of urgency allows dangerous teacher reflections. The first is the belief that personally successful metacognitive skills are generalizable to all students. The second is confidence that personal preferences are sufficient for designing pedagogical activities. The third is a conviction that reform suggestions demand the use of a simple checklist sequence. The last happens when the teacher interprets occurrences, such as minimal student participation or formal parental complaints, as resistance rather than confusion.

Unchallenged, the gap between reform objectives and status-quo realities will remain imperceptible. Reflective distortion can crystalize one's self-concept. To illustrate, consider Mr. Jones's failure to recognize the energy being exerted to rationalize and sustain current practices. Or, Ms. VandenBerg's propensity to generate quick, apparently profound solutions. The issue, Drapeau (2014) noted, is the propensity for status-quo thinking to systematically extinguish an individual's desire to cultivate creative dispositions such as fluency (generating many ideas), originality (narrowing brainstormed options to an innovative solution), flexibility (implementing change), and elaboration (leveraging contextual data to adjust/enhance the implemented change).

The Societal Need for Creativity and Change

A nominal creative disposition minimizes a teacher's efforts to transform educational practices. Unfortunately, societal changes during the last few decades have magnified status-quo risks. Chen (2010) wrote about the impact of technology on student expectations. Far-reaching internet access allows immediate access to a wide range of media venues, interpersonal communication platforms, and open-admission educational programs. The effect is a growing expectation that teachers should honor each student's interests, passions, and biases. In this new reality, allowing students to choose what, when, where, and how to learn is emerging as nonnegotiable while instruction focusing on memorization and replication drifts into obsolescence.

The technological revolution supports the demise of teacher as content expert and the emergence of the teacher as erudite co-learner (Palmer, 1998). The new reality acknowledges that the exponential availability of information is creating a reality where student brains are incapable of possessing all the facts needed to solve a problem. A shift in focus directs the teacher/co-learner to employ authentic, problem-solving methodologies that synthesize content comprehension with skill development metacognition. Outcomes stress a collaborative process where an expanding awareness of problem-specific knowledge gaps direct a systematic approach to uncovering, evaluating, and applying a myriad of content-rich sources (Chen, 2010).

Daggett (2012) combines problem-solving instruction with Common Core Standards. Attentiveness to critical thinking, creativity, and wisdom components result in appropriate student assignments such as:

Asia's growing economic prosperity is increasing the region's number of licensed cars by 25% per year. At this rate, the current road system will reach its capacity in 2025. Projections for accessibility of energy suggest that each year the region will be able to secure 10% fewer barrels of oil. You have been commissioned by local business leaders to determine (1) the probable impact the Asian growth patterns will have on area employment, (2) a risk aversion strategy to ensure our community's continued economic stable, and (3) a proposal to leverage Asian growth as a means of improving our community's prosperity.

The open-ended nature of this task clearly prevents the use of memorization/repetition-based pedagogy. Even more problematic is the task's reliance on integrated cross-disciplinary knowledge and skills. Teachers committed to providing students with support realize the importance of advancing their skill levels in the areas of pedagogy, error analysis, language instruction, and metacognitive skill support.

Implementing the fluid curriculum requires progressive dispositions: Facets include rejecting formulaic practices and embracing ambiguity; resisting the natural tendency to teach as they have been taught; addressing individual needs by making accommodations, adaptations and modifications; replacing a teaching strategy the moment its ineffectiveness becomes apparent; leveraging intrinsic incentives to overcome task risks; and enjoying a personal vocational pilgrimage that encompasses artistic abilities to find and create awe in all learning settings (Bellanca and Brandt, 2010; Darling-Hammond, 2006, 2010; Dewey, 1916; Hennessey, 2015; Marzano, 2010).

Fostering a Positive Cognitive Script

Protecting and nurturing the optimistic teacher/co-learner vision is challenging. Geopolitical entities can quickly overwhelm a classroom-learning environment. For example, the desire to improve student achievement propelled politicians to pass the No Child Left Behind accountability expectations that rewarded high test scores and punished stagnant or dropping scores. Yet, beneath the published test scores, questionable practices such as asking low-performing students to stay home on the high-stakes testing dates were discovered. Darling-Hammond (2010) wondered if the true message of educational reform is actually rooted in a desire to make stakeholders happy rather than offer each child the education they needed.

Researchers at the Arbinger Institute (2010) studied the characteristics of self-deception. Defining characteristics include the tendency to support and justify one's position through the cognitive manipulation of experiences. The goal is to secure feelings of satisfaction and happiness by dismissing sensations of pain or anguish through the use of schemas that employ self-righteous logic. Self-deceptions occur along a continuum. The passive-aggressive end is marked by the appearance of collegiality and the covert antipathy toward opponents. The aggressive end of the continuum consists of open hostility, which is apparent in body language, words, or organized efforts to discredit adversaries.

Regardless of the individual's continuum location, the desire to be right pushes one to fixate on one's own brilliance. The more one pushes, the more difficult it is to see value in others. The self-centered perspective promotes a worldview where the desire to be right is more important than doing right (Arbinger Institute, 2010).

Left unchecked, the self-deceptive cognitive script seeks evidence that affirms personal biases. Transformation occurs through honest, humble reflection. The process starts with an objective appraisal of personal strengths and virtues as well as current responsibilities and constraints. Care is taken to identify and comprehend past behavioral missteps. The aim is to avoid the security found in justification and instead discern the manner in which personal beliefs and actions are contributing to the current state of affairs. Successful self-examination is marked by continuous growth and a positive proactive view of life (Murrell, Diez, Feiman-Nemser, and Schussler, 2010; Palmer, 1998; Wilkerson and Lang, 2007).

Application of the other-centric cognitive script expands the teacher's level of responsibility. Collaborative, interdisciplinary professional relationships are established to break down the silo effect of academic disciplines. Conceptual learning is embraced as the best means to understand the integrated nature of the world. Offering task flexibility is employed to improve student work habits. Deliberately recognizing and certifying student success is adopted as the venue to deliver motivation support (Bellanca and Brandt, 2010; Grant, Strong, Xu, Popp, Sun, and Little, 2014).

Transitioning to Student-Focused Instruction

Implementing collaborative planning and peer-observation protocols, which focus on identifying potential student difficulties and discerning best-practice student support, seems to offer a path toward better twenty-first-century instruction. This assumption, however, is challenged in Grant et. al.'s (2014) comparative study of expert Chinese and U.S. teachers. The issue is the current practice of providing U.S. teachers with less than one-tenth the time that Chinese educators are given to collaboratively plan during the school day. To compensate, the U.S. teachers typically prepare lessons on their own time. The resulting lesson plans are less proactive but do allow teachers the freedom to rapidly respond to student learning difficulties.

The high-stakes, customary practice of basing U.S. teacher performance proficiency on instructional delivery and student behavior reinforces individual lesson planning. Self-sufficiency increases the probability that the rewards for efficient instructional delivery and active student participation are achieved. The assumption, by all involved, that "mind-on" engagement flows from well-behaved, school-appropriate mannerisms allows learning achievement data to drift into the background. Villa, Thousand, and Nevin (2013) argued that barring a major paradigm shift, the false positives generated within these status-quo practices will persist.

Knight (2018) hypothesized that agitating a work-based self-concept with perceptions of failure can diminish agency. Change, Knight argued, requires action steps such as employing positive self-talk, setting goals, connecting mistakes to growth, and monitoring emotional stability. The Arbinger Institute (2010) cautioned against viewing change dispositions as a linear endeavor. Achieving profound change, they contended, requires managing many complex, interrelated variables that make up the individual's cognitive script. Achieving change will require personal metacognition reflections that make unconscious emotions conscious, private preferences public, and intuitive judgments intentional and routine actions deliberate.

Seeking Transformation: The Teacher as Learner

Goodwin, Gibson, Lewis, and Rouleau (2018) asserted that change-embracing equilibrium require collaborative, creative, investigative, and innovative tools. Sousa (2017) theorized that personally rewarding learning entails emotional investment. Knowles, Holton, and Swanson (2015) suggested that generating powerful adult learning necessitates anagogical principles such as providing a clear reason, offering flexibility to self-direct, encouraging application of prior experiences, connecting material to a current life situation, arranging opportunities to increase competency levels, and respecting unique internal motivators. Combined, the ideas suggest that book studies and "sit-and-get" development workshops will not work.

Creating an atmosphere for powerful learning will require understanding and leveraging the organization's culture. The process starts with attentiveness to the vast array of multigenerational interpretations and reactions to reform mandates. Awareness normalizes the diverse population's tendency to overlook the self-sacrificing prerequisite that undergirds efforts to promote harmony, uniformity, and collegiality. The range of perspectives further diverges with pragmatic interpretations of concepts such as personal responsibility and accountability (Lovely and Buffum, 2007).

This foundational understanding supports the identification and employment of transformational strategies. The process begins when the leader carefully transitions discussions from right/wrong debates into dynamic professional dialogs. Intentional steps are enacted to ensure that each participant feels like a valuable contributor. Tensions between efficient use of time and the messy, unpredictable aspects of consensus are resolved through a meditative review and evaluation of three critical professional attributes (Gruenert and Whitaker, 2015; Lovely and Buffum, 2007).

The first professional quality is a pledge to personally adopt the organization's shared vision as the basis for personal growth. Blending individual dreams with the shared vision allows alignment among goals, policies, procedures, and activities. Unity minimizes disagreements as resolutions are framed and evaluated based on the vision's parameters. It is not about being politically correct. It is about the artistic illumination of being sensitive and validating individual contributions, as well as acquiring a devotion for healing and delighting in the shared mission (Darling-Hammond, 2006, 2010; Deal and Kennedy, 1982; DuFour and Marzano, 2011; Hargreaves and Fullan, 2009; Thomas and Inkson, 2009).

The second professional element is a commitment to view others through a strengths-based lens. Mutual respect promotes supportive replies to recognizable differences within cognitive processing preferences, interpersonal communication patterns, task adoption/completion penchants and moral/ethical beliefs. Discovering opportunities to humbly work with others emerges as the individual moves from a self-serving assessment of their strengths, through a self-affirming talent phase, and finally into a strengths-based existence where their created uniqueness is leveraged in a manner that blesses others (Darling-Hammond, 2006, 2010; Liesveld and Miller, 2005; Sternberg, 2006; Thomas and Inkson, 2009).

The third professional trait is a vow to embrace collaborative, mutually respectful pursuits. The competitive and individualistic nature of U.S. culture will challenge the leader's ability to create a collaborative environment. Focusing on the shared vision as well as the strengths-based disposition will mitigate many of the cultural forces. Persistence is needed as participants experience the difference between equal/same and equitable/inclusive relationships. Efficiency and productivity will improve as collaborative practices leverage each individual's giftedness. The outcome will be sustained energy throughout the unpredictable change-oriented journey (Csikszentmihalyi, 1997; Darling-Hammond, 2006, 2010; Thomas and Inkson, 2009).

The Power of Professional-Development Inquiry

The review of holistic development and adult learning theories reminds Dr. Martinez to carefully pace and scaffold the adopted, reform-oriented changes. Dr. Martinez is fully aware that a disproportionate emphasis on the teacher's pedagogical beliefs, instructional tasks, or evidential deliverables may result in the type of cognitive script dissidence that will generate a self-deceptive, status-quo acceptance response. Fortunately, Dr. Martinez understands the power of collaborative, professional-development inquiry.

Danielson (2015) developed an approach to collaborative dialogues. Her process recommends forming dyads based on diverse, educator expertise. Using proficiency progressions, the pair is encouraged to evaluate self-selected, personal data to determine next-step actions. The goal is to provide a tool that assists the novice in mastering pedagogical skills while simultaneously pushing the expert to deeper levels of cognitive understanding. The process is tempered by the framework's use of rubrics, where summative language implicitly promotes high-risk accountability perceptions.

Linking expertise to a rubric location also has the potential to reinforce a destination mentality. Problems emerge when developmental growth is perceived to be limited by nature. Dweck (2006) postulated that an unsatisfactory level of performance will be addressed with a currently established mind-set. The "fix" mind-set generalizes the present situation as inflexible, thus pushing an individual to seek emotional resolution through acquiescence to personal ability or blame to uncontrollable outside forces. Conversely, the growth mind-set will maintain a perception that effort, perseverance, and resilience offer a path toward an eventual return to positive, life improvements.

Sternberg's (2006) theory of successful intelligence complements the mind-set theory. According to Sternberg, brain function is built on the interaction of three distinct abilities: practical, creative, and analytical. Individuals have fixed capacity within each ability area.

However, individuals can learn to use strength in one area to compensate for limitations in another. The malleable nature of the brain allows mentors to assist intellectual growth by: (a) identifying the sets of abilities one uses to obtain success; (b) detecting the method one uses to select environments in which to spend time; and (c) leveraging the purposeful uses of an intellectual profile as the foundation for new problem-solving activities.

A synthesis of holistic development theory, growth mind-set, and successful intelligence has led to the development of the Expanding Environments Teacher Development Framework Matrix (EETDFMatrix). A careful examination of the matrix (see Figure 2.1) underscores a "less is more" ideology. The objective is to provide a set of overarching descriptions that serves as a starting point for inquiry-based, "what-if" dialogues.

EXPANDING ENVIRONMENTS TEACHER DEVELOPMENT FRAMEWORK MATRIX

Context will Generate a Spiraling Effective that will Prevent Linear Skill Development

	Focus is on the Teacher who is the Expert		Focus is on the Class as a Cohesive Unit		Focus is on Individual and Collective Dynamics
SUMMARIZING ESSENCE OF THE COLUMN	Delivering Lessons	Presenting Information	Encouraging Understanding	Assisting in the Discovery of Meaning	Nurturing the Pursuit of Wisdom
SUPPORTING STUDENT ENGAGEMENT IN LEARNING	Urging students to sit quietly and complete the required tasks	Building a classroom community that supports content-focused learning	Fostering inter- and intra-personal content-based interactions	Reinforcing each student's depth of learning through the implementation of individual/classroom monitoring strategies	Facilitating differentiated instruction that enhances each student's current perspective of the world
MANAGING THE ASSESS-PLAN-IMPLEMENT CYCLE	Planning and delivering a content-focused lesson	Employing best-practice strategies that foster active student involvement throughout a content-focused learning segment	Engaging students in context-sensitive, content-based learning	Applying evidence related to each student's strengths and struggles throughout the assess-plan-implement cycle	Embracing learning opportunities that allow flexible and fluid engagement with each student's interests and needs
MAINTAINING A POSITIVE CLASSROOM ENVIRONMENT	Keeping students from disrupting the lesson	Convincing students to participate in planned lesson activities	Responding to off-task behaviors with the goal of reengaging students in content-based learning	Adjusting lesson activities in a manner that supports each student's engagement in learning	Attending to each student's social, moral, and emotional developmental needs as a means of advancing positive citizenship skills
IDENTIFYING AND REFLECTING ON FOUNDATIONAL PERSPECTIVES	Sustaining pedagogical practices with references to personal experiences	Connecting pedagogical practices to educational authorities	Exploring and considering a variety of pedagogical perspectives	Identifying and addressing gaps between personal pedagogical perspectives and actions	Using wisdom to identify and employ actions that fully coordinates personal pedagogical perspectives with leadership activities

Figure 2.1. Expanding Environments Teacher Development Framework Matrix. *Credit:* Dr. Keith Walters, original creation.

Reading from the bottom up, the first row promotes wisdom conversations that link the participant's current knowledge with their value-driven choices. The second row fosters reflection on the relationship between the classroom's microcosm realities and the teacher's management plan. The third row urges discussions on the connection between instructional plans and student holistic, developmental needs. The last row requires evidence-based evaluations that uncover the extent to which instruction is positively impacted each learner.

The five columns propose a simple-to-complex progression. Reading from left to right, the first column depicts a teacher as one who systematically moves through a written lesson plan. The second column describes the teacher as one who intentionally strives to ensure that each student is complying with lesson activity expectations. The third column transitions the teacher from a participatory focus into a learning achievement concentration. The fourth column pushes the teacher to consider the full range of pedagogical activity impact on individuals. The last column portrays the teacher as one who possess the commitment, skills, and abilities to apply leadership principles that facilitates each learner's pursuit of truth, beauty, and justice.

The EETDFMatrix's design is deceptive. Rows are not hierarchical, nor are they distinct. To illustrate, a belief that educational expertise is absolute (row 1, column 2) will dictate the type of evidence collected (row 3, column 4). Equally important is the reality that the matrix is not a rigid, linear progression. Consider the opening story where Mr. Jones focused on implementing linear—"thinking up" pedagogy (row 3, column 3). As a result, a team decision to plan and deliver a global, "thinking down," lessons will most likely be implemented in a step-by-step fashion (row 3, column 1). Embracing this dynamic, nonlinear development path will normalize the asymmetrical trek from novice to expert.

Inquiry-Based Professional Learning Communities

Defining Features

Finding time to schedule inquiry-based, process-oriented conversations using the EETDFMatrix is almost impossible. An implementation solution might be found within an established professional learning community

(PLC). Widespread adoption of PLCs during last decade has diluted educator understanding of effective protocols. Jacobs and Yendol-Hoppey (2010) described a vibrant PLC as a formal gathering of dedicated educators who are collectively striving to use theoretical knowledge and pragmatic tools to refine pedagogical skills, clarify conceptual understandings, and solidify reciprocal relationships. When applied, the PLC offers the team opportunities for problem-solving, risk-taking, and justice-seeking exploration.

The synergetic nucleus of a PLC emerges within the participants' authentic interactions with each other as well as with their situation. Ever-evolving interpersonal relationships compel the members to avoid assessing the team's health based on the actions or efforts of a single individual. Shifting contextual challenges prevent the team from linking effectiveness criteria to a prepackaged evaluation product. Responsive flexibility coupled with entrepreneurial innovation creates the PLC vibrancy that supports the collective and individual learning needs of each team member (Bellanca and Brandt, 2010; DuFour and Marzano, 2011; Hargreaves and Fullan, 2009; Palmer, 1998, 2000).

The PLC collaborative must be carefully nurtured. Lack of action step clarity specificity, new activity implementation mistakes, and diverse worldview misunderstandings each have the potential to create tensions. Unaddressed, conflicts will materialize. Active listening can reduce interpersonal strains and establishes an atmosphere of trust. Trust supplants individualism with a devotion to interdependence. *Trust allows one to give the benefit of the doubt.* Finally, trust provides one with the courage to take the type of risks associated with transformational reform (Bellanca and Brandt, 2010; DuFour and Marzano, 2011; Hargreaves and Fullan 2009; Palmer, 1998, 2000).

Transitioning the idea of PLCs into an effective practice starts with a SWOT (strengths-weakness-opportunity-threat) analysis. The first step articulates and celebrates the site's core values and traditions. Areas of concern are then used to generate inquiry questions. Assigning team members inquiry responsibilities distributes leadership and increases collaborative participation. Care is taken to design an inquiry cycle that is between one semester and one academic year, as that diminishes the short-cycle stress and long-cycle apathy (Deal and Kennedy, 1982; DuFour and Marzano, 2011; Goodwin, Gibson, Lewis, and Rouleau, 2018; Gruenert and Whitaker, 2015; Hargreaves and Fullan, 2009).

Completion of the SWOT provides the framework under which the PLC team will function. Topic freedom makes the process relevant. A broad five-step implementation process guides the team. Step 1 focuses on differentiating symptoms (what is seen) from problems (the underlying elements to be addressed). Two strategies help the team achieve an appropriate depth of analysis. In immediate agreement situations, the group will ask, "why do you think we see this?" five successive times. In frustration, nonagreement circumstances, the consensus process is employed. A synthesis with the SWOT analysis helps determine if a venture outside the team's comfort zone is needed (DuFour and Marzano, 2011).

With the potential solution's parameters defined, the team examines research related to the science (theory) and the art (practice) of learning. Care is taken to read studies that consider new practices and alleviate fears of the unknown. Research study dialogs will examine factual material, conceptual schema that link the study's thesis to current understandings, procedures that connect the research with practice, strategies for implementation, and the manner in which the study's bias coordinates or conflicts with team member values. The conclusion of step 2 is a summary report that highlights discoveries and articulates the extent to which application of the findings will require changing current professional practices (DuFour and Marzano, 2011).

Step 3 synthesizes the team's unique, site-based cultural context with the step two research summary. A critical task is upholding the team's nonnegotiable values. This focus is important because inquiry questions can generate significant excitement and lead some team members astray. Teams can resist excessive cognitive inquiry by maintaining a clear focus on the needs of students, assigning specific implementation tasks to each member, and setting specific completion dates that include clear consequences for missing deadlines. Prior to enacting the plan, an evaluation system will be developed that verifies the extent to which the plan is helping the team solve the step one problem (DuFour and Marzano, 2011).

Step 4, the implementation phase, will increase team member stress. Mutual reminders of the EETDFMatrix's fluid proficiency premise and growth mind-set assurances can calm emotions. The key element in making the plan's impact explicit is gathering data from sources such as test score error analyses, homework submission percentages, parent interviews, student surveys, or formal classroom observations. Initial data sets must be immediately evaluated for reliability, validity, and sufficiency. Any identified data gap should be instantly addressed. Critical evaluation will assist the team in managing gaps between the research study's promises and the implementation realities (DuFour and Marzano, 2011).

Step 5 addresses the end of the inquiry cycle. Positive step 4 data will generate a synergetic energy that will propel the team to continue culture-changing experimentation. Negative step 4 data will be frustrating and may nudge members toward self-preservation or self-deception reactions. A nurturing, trust-assured team can support a member's emotional struggles. Addressing the negative emotional spiral requires members to refocus attention on envisioning the positive outcomes that the next inquiry cycle may bring. In essence, the goal is to build a culture that confronts initial interpretations of data by subjecting one's own ideas to alternative interpretations (Brackett and Simmons, 2015; DuFour and Marzano, 2011; Knight, 2018)

Supporting, Monitoring, and Encouraging

Moving individuals outside their comfort zone will yield a wide variety of responses. For some, the view continuity and safety will be removed. For others, the positive self-concept rooted in the ability to complete well-defined tasks with perfection will be challenged. PLC leadership must provide the anxious teachers with support. Aguilar (2013) suggested transformational coaching which involves assigning a nonsupervisory individual to the struggling teacher. Counseling sessions are informal and provide space to explore the multifaceted interrelationships that may be confounding the teacher's ability to embrace change. The challenge to this approach is finding money to hire the coach and provide classroom release time.

The busy lives of school administrators demand that inquiry-based PLCs be self-sustaining. Team leaders must arise from within. Union contracts and site-based politics can propel the wrong person into the lead position. One solution is to adopt the concept of leadership. Leadership emerges when individuals identify, accept, and embrace personal responsibility to successfully complete all assigned tasks with minimal oversight (Jackson and Parry, 2011).

The challenge with the leadership concept is supporting the skills and knowledge growth necessary to make wise decisions. Multiple classroom observations can enhance participant understandings. Kachur, Stout, and Edwards (2013)recommend using classroom walkthroughs. The establishment of common protocols for scheduling, observing, gathering data, and offering feedback are foundational to the walkthrough strategy. The best walkthroughs allow colleagues the opportunity to observe other team members implementing the inquiry cycle's step four plan. Seeing a colleague experiencing similar successes and struggles generates a shared schema that enriches conversations. Once again, the issue is finding money for classroom release time.

Providing support during each step of the inquiry-based PLC process requires securing time. In step 1, the principal needs time to identify and mentor resistive teachers. Failure to listen and support the resistor increase the probability that negative thoughts will be spread throughout the school. In step 2, team members require some relief from the time pressures associated with typical responsibilities such as grading papers, examining test scores, planning lessons, and talking to parents. Without relief, the ability to complete in-depth research will dissipate (Glickman, 2002; Hargreaves and Fullan, 2009).

In step 3, the principal must have time to review the team's work and the team must have time to make necessary revisions. A cursory review or rushed revisions may compromise the plan's ability to quantitatively monitoring the impact on student performance. In step 4, the principal must have time to encourage and revitalize team members when the implemented plan transitions from new and exciting to routine. Without specific praise and detailed challenge questions team members will revert to pre-reform routines. Finally, in step 5, team members and principals require time to nurture the type of trust that gives others the benefit of the doubt, forgives gaffes, and celebrates success (Glickman, 2002; Hargreaves and Fullan, 2009).

Creative First Steps

Dr. Martinez's review of the inquiry-based PLC model left her a little discouraged. Where was she going to find the time? How could she transition the math team from traditional practices (we have always done things this way) into reform-embracing, student-focused approaches? Sitting quietly at her desk, Dr. Martinez remembered Ms. Kumar's behavior during the meeting. Though not a vocal participant, Ms. Kumar's facial and body language expressions suggested that she was not content with the memorization/repetition plan. Dr. Martinez slowly mused about approaches she could propose that would excite Ms. Kumar and possibly launch the beginning of a math department transformation.

An examination of contemporary educational practices offers Dr. Martinez three options. The first is leveraging the preparation period. A dynamic teacher rarely wastes this time. However, those desiring to improve their skills may be open to using some of this time for professional development. Strategies might include (1) adding the teacher to the program improvement accreditation sub-team, (2) partnering two or more teachers with shared dispositions but different content area expertise to examine topics such as problem-based learning, and (3) asking the teacher to prepare a staff-development presentation that focuses on a small element of a reform such as integrating socioemotional development principles into classroom management plans.

The second potential strategy involves technology. The national and state mathematics associations have well-developed websites and regularly scheduled professional-development associations. Networking within the association will provide a list of educators who are committed to inquiry-based, reformed-oriented growth. Using web-based platforms such as Google Docs and Zoom, teachers from different sites can engage in lesson studies, video observations, and even low-level co-teaching.

The final approach involves partnering with a local university. Low-level cooperation would involve welcoming a student teacher into your classroom. Co-planning, co-teaching, and video studies will deepen cognitive understandings as well as alert each participant to potential gaps between theoretical intentions and actual classroom practices. Mid-level cooperation would be opening your school site for a research study. University expectations for publications leave many professors scrambling for sites. Partnering also opens opportunities for grants. Finally, high-level cooperation would entail a formal lab school partnership. These are hard to establish; but a review of Dewey's (1916) work highlights the creative and transformation possibilities.

SUMMARY

The world is rapidly changing. Technology allows individuals across vast geographic distances to interact on a regular basis. Technology also provides rapid and expansive amounts of knowledge to be transmitted in seconds. Preparing children to thrive in this technological environment is a major priority for most educators. Yet change is difficult. Participants often possess cognitive scripts controlled by status-quo preferences.

Envisioning powerful, transformational twenty-first-century education requires differentiating between memorization/repetition and problem-based/collaborative pedagogies. Compounding the instructional confusion is the practice of educational entrepreneurs reformatting status-quo pedagogical practices using modern technology. Discerning the hidden curriculum agendas is difficult. Fortunately, the inquiry-based PLC model provides a systematic approach to engaging educators in professional growth.

Leaders seeking to implement inquiry-based PLC protocols must be patient, persistent, and innovative. Holistic development theory alerts leaders to the slow, systematic approach that adults require to learn new information. The fluid ebbs and flows of mastery and discovery require replacing destination learning with pilgrimage discovery. The tensions between providing time for professional learning and current school routines require outside-the-box solutions. Given the dynamic, rapidly evolving realities, it is clear that the formula for future educational success is not a rigid set of steps but rather a dynamic, strength-based, collaboration. Change is hard, but failure to change will be even more debilitating. The choice is ours.

Chapter Three

The BIG ASK

James Freemyer

PRE-READING REFLECTION

1. Why have attempts at teaching mathematics in a real-life, problem-based approach been so unsuccessful over the years?
2. How do mathematics departments excite more students to continue taking advanced courses?
3. How difficult is it for mathematics to change their teaching approach so that students understand advanced-level concepts?
4. What is the best focus for academic leaders to improve mathematics test scores?

WHAT TO EXPECT IN THIS CHAPTER

The goal today is to better engage students of all ability levels to such an extent that they become excited about mathematics courses and choose to take advanced courses in the STEM arena. The new focus is to engage more students with more in-depth understanding of key concepts by asking them more challenging questions. One title for this challenging approach has been termed "productive struggle."

Yet to ask students, who often have an aversion to mathematics, to engage in more challenging work is a lot to ask. As hard as it is for students to change, it is even more challenging to ask mathematics teachers to completely adapt their instructional approach to accommodate this new conceptual tactic. It is, in fact, a BIG ASK of mathematics teachers and students!

Yet schools continue to initiate change like we are asking teachers to teach a different curriculum. This is far more complicated than teaching a new curriculum. It involves a different paradigm as we seek to engage students of all academic levels to engage in intense, conceptually oriented tasks that stretch their resolve and cognitive abilities. Teachers are asking students to participate in theoretical discourse that critiques theirs and others work, provides analysis of right and wrong responses, and making sense of multifaceted ideas. Increasing profitable discourse for significant learning is a concept that is easier to promote than to execute effectively.

THE ROLE OF THE PRINCIPAL IN PROMOTING CONCEPTUAL LEARNING

If schools desire to seek such radical change, the principals must become intimately involved in the process and supportive of the teachers. Schools in Europe and Asia that have been successfully initiating such significant change have provided significant support for teachers. This support must include more time for collaboration with each other (a) for planning lessons, (b) observing each other teach, and (c) debriefing after lessons (Freemyer, 2018).

In addition, teachers need principals' encouragement and support as they explore ways to challenge conceptual understanding for our best and brightest students, our average students, and below-average students at the same time in the same classroom. Such a significant paradigm shift necessitates extended planning to design lessons that challenge all students and help them all arrive at conceptual understanding. In order to guide each student to conceptual awareness, productive struggle must be prevalent, and the importance of individual student mistakes must be considered a natural product of a more engaged classroom.

Change Expected

Mathematics teachers worldwide have been asked to make major changes in their pedagogical approach to teaching. This new approach is dramatically different from the way they have learned the subject and the ways they have taught their students for years. Asking teachers to reengineer their entire approach to teaching is certainly a big ask. Should we require a major change like this devoid of proper assistance, encouragement, and support? It is even more of a challenge than asking a baby boomer to be fluent in Chinese in a couple of months.

To be clear, the goal is to increase the number of students of all ability levels who decide to continue taking the challenging courses of upper-level mathematics and science classes. The potential rewards are substantial. Many of the better-paying jobs require graduates who have the requisite background that STEM courses provide. Motivating teenagers to tackle these courses with the hope of an eventual payday is indeed a challenge.

First, teachers must take courses that students already find difficult and redesign them to take students to a more in-depth conceptual level of understanding preparing students for future courses that also increase in difficulty. In other words, we must make hard courses even more taxing. At the same time, mathematics teachers are being asked to motivate students of all ability levels to agree to voluntarily accept such rigor. The only carrot available to mathematics teachers is the hope that the efforts of teens will pay off with good jobs half a decade later; it is well known that this is an unusual realization in the adolescent brain. Therefore, the motivation must be more from immediate rewards accompanying daily comprehension than futuristic goals.

As mathematics teachers are redesigning pedagogical approaches to teach conceptual knowledge that prepares for advanced content, they must also find ways to engage all students from varying ability levels while motivating them to aspire to continue taking courses that tax personal abilities to the limits. Brighter students must learn the challenges of more conceptual understanding in earlier high school courses so they become accustomed to productive struggles that await in the upper-level courses. Otherwise they assume that, when mathematics starts to tax their understanding, they have reached their limits.

Helping Students Persevere

However, if students become accustomed to being stretched with new concepts, they are already acclimated to persevering through the challenge. In fact they embrace the challenge. Average and below-average students must experience enough success with more challenging problems during earlier years in high school to entice them to continue the sense of accomplishment in the later years of high school.

Teachers are being asked to unleash their passion for mathematics and their enthusiasm for their work so students can tap into that energy to fuel a love of mathematics. This is a big ask. It cannot be done by teachers who are trapped in the insolation of their own classroom left to work out the details alone and at the expense of the precious little time available to love and nurture their own personal families.

The Need for Leadership Involvement

Academic leaders must intervene. Math scores will not increase because top-down initiatives designed to place the burden on local math teachers. Only with a collaborative effort, which includes leaders rolling up their sleeves with the teachers and providing guidance, support, encouragement, and resources, will math scores begin to compete with those in other countries. Math teacher collaboration and support found in the better schools in Europe and Asia provide a blueprint for this book and real hope for motivating more students to consider STEM careers. Remembering the failed attempts in the United States to change mathematics approaches in the 1960s, 1980s, and early 2000s enforces the need for more substantive, long-lasting change.

Now the focus is on exploring ways for mathematics teachers to recruit more students from all levels of academic ability to choose more courses in this content area. You heard that right. The goal is to take one of the most challenging subjects in the high school curriculum and motivate more students to work harder to understand complex issues throughout the high school years. How can this be done?

The uniform consensus around the world is surprising. Teaching at a higher level through a more conceptual approach is essential in order for more students to continue in this subject. That makes sense. This requires increased student engagement in productive struggle, authentic problem solving, inquiry, and student discourse. If that is not enough, we also want to include students considered to be average or below average in ability in previous math courses and motivate them to continue taking these challenging courses. Carol Dweck's (2016) framework provides the underpinnings that demonstrate how we can utilize a growth mind-set to reach all students.

Engaging Students through Productive Struggle

The game plan is to take students who previously found mathematics dull and boring and motivate them to work harder, engaging them in more challenging approaches to learning mathematics at a higher level. Recent research in Indiana, Ireland, Great Britain, South Korea, and Japan tell a helpful story of just how this can and has been done. More academic rigor when accompanied by student engagement and productive struggle can move the study of mathematics from disjointed and boring to challenging and rewarding. We must emphasize the rewards that lie ahead in careers in the STEM arena. However, such a dramatic change in instructional approach calls for dramatic assistance from the school leadership team.

Motivating young people to tackle difficult challenges has a precedent. There are many students who begin college as premedical majors every year, knowing that a limited number will be accepted in medical school. Yet students understand the challenges before them and embrace the challenge. The rewards can be substantial in the STEM arena as well. More and better-paying jobs await those who can complete the work. What is holding us back?

We must have effective teachers to approach their jobs through research-driven practices that excite and help students succeed. We need teachers who are adept at helping students in learning mathematics. We need significant change. We also must have the help of the local principal. We must have teachers with passion for the content. A conviction that all students learn and love the beauty of mathematics is essential. But students require more than that.

The teachers who learn to adjust teaching to engage all students and who are willing to provide extra assistance and encouragement can indeed make a positive difference in more young people's lives. Unfortunately, teachers must better understand a new approach to teaching. They then need the time to try new approaches and learn firsthand how to make them work. Our students need to experience more than the one or two effective mathematics teachers common in most schools.

A Worldwide Change Initiative

If, as an American teacher, you are feeling the pressure of improving math test scores, you should take comfort in the fact that teachers around the world are being asked to significantly change their teaching approaches. In Ireland, a nationwide change initiative began in 2010 with a focus to retrain every single mathematics teacher in a three-year process. This new initiative to teach more conceptually, as well as procedurally, continues today. In Great Britain, a similar process is occurring with the goal of encouraging a greater number of students to consider careers in STEM areas.

In Asia, South Korea, and Japan, academic leaders continue to retrain teachers to take a more student-centered pedagogical approach, vastly different from their stereotypical, lecture-driven past. Asian teachers are making an even more extensive pedagogical change than teachers in the United States. In the past, Japanese faculty lectured from their platform behind a podium. Classes observed in 2018 were characterized by the teacher off the platform coaching students working in groups. Countries that motivate their mathematics teachers to succeed in such a transformative change and engage all students in learning mathematics will have the inside track on the technological global jobs of the future. Japanese teachers spend more time guiding student learning than lecturing on platform. See figure 3.1.

Figure 3.1. Japanese teacher helping students learn on their level. *Credit:* Nathan Freemyer, graphic artist

Mathematicians worldwide concur that teaching using authentic problem solving, a focus on student engagement and inquiry, and student discourse will provide more students of all academic levels who succeed and continue in STEM courses. However, asking teachers to embrace yet another new teaching approach, when they have taught and were taught mathematics with a different focus, is indeed a big ask. If teachers are to successfully encourage students of different academic ability levels to continue to study mathematics and STEM-related courses, they must cast a wider net.

NCTM Leads the Way

The National Council of Teachers of Mathematics (NCTM) has provided a host of supporting materials and a blueprint for how mathematics teachers should approach their courses differently. This approach is focused on generating (a) conceptual understanding, (b) procedural fluency, (c) strategic competence, (d) adaptive reasoning, and (e) productive disposition create mathematical proficiency (National Research Council, 2001, as cited in *Principles to Actions*, 2014). Providing sound pedagogical materials is only a good first step. Asking mathematics teachers to make such significant changes in their approach to teaching is something totally different.

This chapter will provide educational leaders with a short outline that could be used as a framework from which to work; later chapters will discuss how high schools throughout the country can actually invest in improving scores. The major focus of this book, based on research conducted in the United States, Europe, and Asia, is to make the case that to actually achieve results, school districts must invest in mathematics teachers, providing time and opportunities for collaboration or the United States will fall behind other countries in the quest to drive economic growth through STEM advances. If it has worked in those areas around the world, it can work in the United States, too. The following material is provided in a way to allow school leadership to understand the needed support that is necessary to allow the United States to compete on a global stage.

NCTM Materials Designed to Help

One resource that effectively outlines the degree to which mathematics teachers are being asked to adjust their teaching approach follows. A short summary of NCTM's book, *Principles to Actions*, follows in an effort to assist academic leaders in understanding the degree to which mathematics teachers are being asked to redesign their current teaching approach. This summary provides local principals and mathematics teachers with a clearer look at the degree to which change is being required and hopefully helps make the case for increases in teacher planning time, teacher collaboration, substantial help, and encouragement as mathematics teachers overhaul their current pedagogy.

Principles to Actions (2014) summarizes the focus of this book by explicitly stating that "the core of the research-informed practices is offered as a framework for strengthening the teaching and learning of mathematics. The first step is to study and begin to understand the changes that are needed. The next step involves educators collectively and collaboratively supporting one another" (p. 57) as they learn to change the current paradigm. The book was not designed for teachers working in isolation and attempting to make major progress in their teaching approach. If principals provide time for teacher collaboration and experimentation, they stand to reap dramatic increases in students prepared for STEM careers.

THE BLUEPRINT FOR CONCEPTUAL
LEARNING IN MATHEMATICS

In *Principles to Actions* (2014), NCTM provides a clear blueprint for this change initiative. Learners must:

- Engage with challenging tasks
- Connect new learning with prior knowledge
- Acquire conceptual knowledge
- Construct knowledge socially, through discourse
- Receive descriptive and timely feedback
- Develop metacognitive awareness

In *Principles to Actions* (2014), NCTM provides teachers with a solid framework to engage all students throughout the lesson. To accomplish the goals within a particular school culture requires a great amount of work. It is one thing to tell teachers to "prompt student interaction and discourse" (p. 10); it is quite another for teachers to accomplish it successfully within any given school culture. Therefore, teachers need release time to practice the new approaches while collaborating with peers. This is what the more effective schools in Japan, South Korea, and Scotland provided for their teachers as they sought to apply the principles in their classrooms.

There are no shortcuts to academic success. The Eight Mathematics Teaching Practices provide a framework that principals, in conjunction with department chairs, can use to develop engaging classes that promote both procedural and conceptual understanding.

Establish Mathematics Goals to Focus Learning

According to *Principles to Actions* (2014), the first of the eight approaches calls for teachers to establish clear goals, situate the goals within learning progressions, and use the goals to guide instructional decisions. Is this not the work of entire departments when adopting new textbooks or realigning curriculum goals? Why do we expect one teacher to accomplish this in her spare time? Where does one find time for this when working on day-to-day lesson planning? Can it even be done effectively without the input of others?

Then the goals must be taught within a framework of learning progressions. This is again the work of mathematics departments and should not be placed upon individual teachers. Connecting goals to the big ideas of mathematics (p. 13) is, in itself, an enormous, time-consuming task. Done effectively, the task calls for serious research and study as teachers refresh upper-level mathematics content and decide on steps in a progression that would lead students to exciting new conclusions that lead eventually to advanced levels. Each school represents a unique school culture that affects the approach to operative learning progressions. These approaches are significantly impacted by the ability of elementary and middle school teacher effectiveness. Teacher collaboration and action research are critical for success.

This task is completed more effectively when one mathematics teacher engages in collaborative dialogue with others. This would require extra joint lesson planning times to enable mathematics teachers to share ideas and plan effective, sequenced lessons. Individual teachers would be charged with designing daily lessons. This understanding provides the opportunity for mathematics teachers to make the appropriate adjustments during instructional lessons, helping students connect key concepts. Principals must invest in teachers' focused growth and understanding if they expect teachers to generate meaningful discourse and improve connections, "supporting students as they struggle" (p. 14). The ASK is simply beyond what individual teachers can accomplish alone, even if they had sufficient planning time. Countries around the world have accepted this premise; but in the United States we have not admitted to ourselves the degree of work we require to make positive strides in helping students engage in productive struggle.

To be fair, NCTM has developed example lessons in *Taking Action* (2017) to assist teachers in applying these ideas. Having examples of ways to accomplish these blatantly challenging new techniques and being able to apply them in a given culture at a particular school are two different things. Even if the materials were written for an urban, suburban, or rural setting, which they are not, the task to apply them in a particular school in any region of the country would still be perplexing. In short, step one is a BIG ASK, and there are seven more steps to consider.

Promoting Reasoning and Problem Solving

Next, *Principles to Actions* (2014) calls for teachers to design "tasks that promote reasoning and problem solving" (p. 17). Since coordinated tasks that promote such reasoning are not yet developed and available for mathematics teachers, there is further need for joint teacher collaboration and experimentation. In five to seven years, when more effective resources become available, the challenge of adapting them to fit the local culture will still remain. The goal of "high level student thinking and reasoning" (p. 17) is a noble goal, but "the most difficult to implement well and are often transformed into less demanding tasks" (p. 17) during the course of everyday instruction.

Tackling such tasks is more complicated than simply designing effective lessons. The few schools observed who were adept at this process in Scotland, Japan, and South Korea have successfully created a culture where students pride themselves in taking on the big challenges and are not deterred when immediate understanding is not attained. Slow progress in those countries came in small steps during five to seven years of focused effort (Freemyer, 2018). Students' sense of identity must revolve around the hunt not just the capture. That is a major cultural change. Perseverance is a coveted by-product of such classrooms. Was it coincidental that such effective schools provided extensive opportunities for teachers' joint collaboration?

While *Principles to Actions* (2014) provides excellent examples of such lessons, not all examples align to middle and high school classes. Such lessons are simply not developed and available yet. Even when they do become available, how much more effective will be lessons devised by local teachers as they grapple with these new approaches personally?

The process of nudging students forward is, in itself, a challenging task. At what point should the teacher insert herself into the process of supporting students in their productive struggle? How much is too much and for which ability level of students? These are pedagogical issues that require constant reflection and debate. One-person debates simply fall short of what is needed to make significant progress.

If the United States is to compete on a global level, we simply must invest time and provide dialogue opportunities for our current mathematics teachers. Teachers must provide opportunities for students to "engage on a regular basis with tasks that focus on reasoning and problem solving and make possible multiple entry points and varied solution strategies" (*Principles to Actions*, 2014, p. 23). Can we expect real progress in this area without much of an investment?

Connecting with Mathematical Representations

The next teaching practice recognized to successfully impact mathematics student learning is the importance of using and connecting to mathematics representation (*Principles to Actions*, 2014, p. 24). "When students learn to represent, discuss, and make connections among mathematical ideas in multiple forms, they demonstrate deeper mathematical understanding and enhance problem-solving abilities" (*Principles to Actions*, 2014, p. 24). Young learners benefit from looking at representations of ideas using graphs, sketches, pictures, charts, and other visuals to support active discourse.

Materials designed to use such visuals to promote dialogue are not available yet. Teachers, beginning to organize in such organizations as Mathematics Teaching Circles, have gained in popularity. Teachers need assistance in designing guides that students can use to utilize with mathematics drawings and visuals to support, explain, and justify their reasoning. According to Clark, Janssen, Harsy, Klanderman, Maxwell, and Robbert (2017), "Many K–12 mathematics teachers are not ready to teach from a conceptual or inquiry-based perspective because they have an algorithmic understanding of mathematics" (p. 23).

This is yet another teaching approach that is not normally part of most mathematics teachers' skill set. Having opportunities within and outside the local school's context are necessary to help teachers effectively use these representations. Teachers need our support.

Facilitating Meaningful Mathematical Discourse

The facilitation of effective mathematical discourse by students of all ability levels is the next component of effective teaching and learning outlined by *Principles to Action* (2014, p. 29). "Reasoning and problem solving are primary mechanisms for developing conceptual understanding" (*Principles to Actions*, 2014, p. 30). They define mathematical discourse to "include purposeful exchange of ideas through classroom discussion as well as through other forms of verbal, visual, and written communication" (p. 29).

This represents another important area in which most teachers have little experience or sufficient time to allow students such time-consuming approaches. According to Carpenter, Franke, and Levi (2003, as cited in *Principles to Action*, 2014), "Students who learn to articulate and justify their own mathematical ideas, reason through their own and others' mathematical explanations, and provide rationale for their answers develop deep understanding that is critical to their future success in mathematics and related fields" (p. 30).

Effective schools in Europe and Asia spend considerable time honing their skills in facilitating meaningful mathematics discourse. In Tokyo, all mathematics classes must be at least fifty minutes in length. Providing either extended class time once a week or additional periods of help is more and more common for schools that are serious about mathematics advancement for all students.

Effective teachers work to create a culture of discourse by building on and honoring student thinking (*Principles to Actions*, 2014, p. 30). This approach takes time. Teachers in Ireland supported the major change initiative, but they were frustrated with expectations of major changes without provision of extended periods of classroom time for students to experience this kind of meaningful discourse. Forty-five-minute classes do not provide ample time to apply the NCTM guidelines.

Posing Purposeful Questions

Questions can be used to encourage students to "explain and reflect on their thinking" (*Principles to Actions*, 2014, p. 35). This is the one component in which current teachers are often proficient. However, teachers must be encouraged to go even deeper into probing responses. In a rush to cover more material, teachers seldom actually ask student their thinking process or have them explain how their approach differs from that of another student. Principals who find ways to provide more teacher/student contact time can positively support classroom questions.

Such questions are even more effective when teachers provide some components of flipping the classroom. By utilizing technology to cover some of the more detailed portions of new material, teachers provide additional time during class to ask more questions and allow students individually and in groups to grapple with conceptual understandings. Working together on this approach was a hallmark of a model school in Scotland.

Build Procedural Fluency from Conceptual Understanding

When one begins with conceptual understanding, the procedural processes seem much less disjointed. Students must "know which procedure is appropriate and most productive in a given situation, what a procedure accomplishes, and what kind of results to expected" (*Principles to Actions*, 2014, p. 42). The emphasis on real conceptual understanding is a new twist for most mathematics teachers.

Worksheets focused on procedural proficiency have been a part of the teaching arsenal for mathematics teachers for decades. Adjusting this focus is an important component that can easily revert to rote work unless group teacher focus overcomes the old cultural norms. According to *Principles to Action*, early work on reasoning pays big dividends when students get to the algebra stage of mathematical understanding. A focus on conceptual understanding in algebra can help with conceptual understanding in calculus.

When students experience a strong conceptual understanding, they are often more effective on standardized test and later high-stakes assessments of student learning. Teachers need to provide students with opportunities to develop reasoning strategies and methods for solving problems (*Principles to Actions*, 2014, p. 47).

Let's be clear. Using conceptual understanding to drive the why and how of procedural mathematical principles takes more classroom time. Teachers who feel constant pressure to keep up with the demands of the curriculum guides and pacing guidelines are quick to compromise this conceptual approach. Telling students rather than preparing lessons helps them discover, is quicker, and is most definitely easier.

Support Productive Struggle

Principles to Actions authors posit that American mathematics teachers are quick to swoop in and help struggling students as they contend with difficult mathematics concepts. If teachers are given both additional time to cover challenging materials and additional time to prepare lessons that incorporate such activities, then students can benefit from productive struggle. Students must learn perseverance, which cannot occur when teachers provide the answers when classroom time is concluding.

Effective teachers realize that the standardized test awaiting each mathematics student is loaded with examples of questions that require problem solving and productive struggle. If students are to learn not to give up, then they need time to grapple with conceptual understanding. Students should learn to explain their work and defend their ideas. They should also be able to critique other students' ideas. Students must learn to value struggle and critique their peers' reasoning. That only happens when teachers make it happen. Teachers can only do this if they have the enough preparation time and delivery time.

Elicit and Use Evidence of Student Thinking

The eighth and final component of effective mathematical teaching and learning involves challenging teachers to elicit and use evidence of student thinking. Teachers must develop proficiencies in assessing student understanding throughout a given lesson and adjust their instruction accordingly. Professors who work with young preservice mathematics teachers often say this is one of the biggest hurdles to effective instruction.

Adjusting instruction on the go is something that often provides a real challenge to new teachers. However, experienced teachers become set in their ways through repeated teaching of the same material over the years so as to inhibit reflection on such approaches. *Principles to Actions* (2014) suggests that teachers must use "high-level tasks to reveal students' thinking and mathematical understanding" (p. 54).

To ensure that teachers consistently secure evidence of student thinking, one school in Scotland required systematic assessment every two weeks at a minimum. Teachers either gave a test or developed a homework assignment where students demonstrated and explained their thinking on course materials. This allowed the teachers to provide extensive feedback to students regularly, helping them to better recognize key concepts and to adjust student understanding. Teachers used that feedback to adjust their teaching.

WHAT IS A PRINCIPAL TO DO?

Provide Increased Planning Time

Principals and academic leaders play a major role in the realignment of mathematics curriculum in an effort to better recruit more students of all academic levels to persevere in successfully completing upper-level mathematics courses. Effective schools in Europe and Asia have provided a clear road map for improved mathematics scores. It begins with allowing mathematics teachers extra time to plan more conceptually oriented lessons. In Ireland, however, a national survey completed by 147 secondary mathematics teachers voiced their frustration with a major new initiative that was devoid of planning time to adequately plan the changes. In a nationwide survey, almost 50 percent of teachers mentioned the need for more planning time.

Personal observations and interviews in Ireland underscored the frustration with major changes and little assistance or time to make the proposed changes. At the same time, schools observed in Scotland told a different story. Principals provided extra time for both individual planning and collaborative designing of lessons. A few of the schools observed had an extra teacher paid by the government. This allows all mathematics teachers extra planning time and time to observe and collaborate with colleagues. When observing those classes, it was clear that lessons had been jointly designed because they were identical from the introductory anticipatory set through the example problems and finally to the group exercises. If college students major in mathematics education in Scotland, they are guaranteed a job by the government even if there are no openings. This makes mathematics education an attractive course of study at university.

In Tokyo, Japan, schools that agree to work on improving their mathematics teaching approach are provided with an additional teacher. This again allows for more time for joint lesson planning and collaborative observations with pedagogical dialogue. An investment in increased planning along with collaborative dialogue can pay huge dividends. The school district in Seoul, South Korea, mimicked this approach to assist teachers with an additional mathematics teacher when requested. Asians have a clear advantage in training more students who can impact new technologies in the future.

Provide for Peer Planning and Joint Observation

Observing classes in Scotland revealed identical lessons being taught by different teachers in some schools. Imagine teaching a lesson while a colleague observes, providing extra eyes to determine what is working and what falls short. A rich discussion that follows the lesson can greatly assist teachers as they grow and learn what it means to teach more conceptually.

The Japanese are known for their Lesson Study approach. That teaching approach allows for joint lesson planning, teaching with numerous teachers observing, often including a specialist from the university, and debriefing as colleagues dialogue about what works with which students and how the lesson could be improved. Demonstrations regarding how this approach works are available at some schools in the United States. The initiative in Ireland has adopted this approach to help mathematics teachers apply the new principles required for a more conceptual approach to teaching mathematics. The greatest help that principals can provide mathematics teachers as they seek to tackle these new teaching approaches is to allow them to work collaboratively with teachers in their own school, in the school district, or within the region.

AP training and collaboration sessions form a model for the type of collaboration that is needed for all middle and high school courses. Teacher dialogue revolving around pedagogical issues is rife with academic benefits. Department-level action research, which was so effective in Scotland, could be the rule rather than the exception in the United States. Principals play a vital role in helping make that happen. If academic leaders are serious about improving mathematics scores and motivating more students to prepare for STEM careers, they can make a real difference in the lives of students.

Provide Increased Student/Teacher Contact Time

Not all courses in a secondary curriculum are created equal. Mathematics and English provide the most significant high-stakes testing. Should there not be more time devoted to improving the scores that make the most difference for students? The number one concern of mathematics teachers in Ireland is that teachers were not given additional classroom time in which to allow for the agreed-upon productive struggle. Students simply cannot grapple with big ideas and conceptual understanding in a forty-five-minute class session. Different goals require different, favorable parameters designed to meet the challenges.

Provide Additional Help and Assistance

Teachers who were recognized as most effective in Indiana were also the teachers who were identified by academic leaders as professionals who provided more extra assistance. They demonstrated a real commitment to helping students succeed. In Scotland, teachers discussed the extra measures they took to help students succeed. They mentioned help sessions during lunch. They talked about taking turns with other teachers to help after school in student help sessions. One exemplary school in Scotland described Saturday sessions where twenty to thirty students sought further

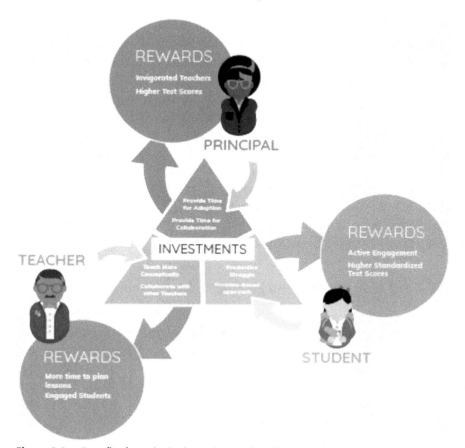

Figure 3.2. Benefits for principal, teacher and student stakeholders for collaboration time provided by the school. *Credit:* Nathan Freemyer, graphic artist

assistance on a regular basis. One teacher allowed students to call them at home each evening between 8 and 9 p.m.

The above diagram illustrates how each stakeholder invests in the proposed changes and how each stands to gain from a focused attempt at improving mathematics instruction.

The ethos of Project Maths was to move away from teacher-centered teaching methodologies that were recognized as being the norm in Irish post-primary classrooms before Project Maths (Gill, 2006; Lyons et al., 2003), toward more constructivist, student-centered, active learning meth-odologies. If we adopt this approach, everyone benefits.

SUMMARY

Asking mathematics teachers to dramatically change their teaching approach is a BIG ASK. Principals must do more than just tell teachers to change. They must help them change. There are no shortcuts to such significant change. Principals will benefit greatly if they find ways to help teachers collaborate and if they can provide more teacher/student contact time.

Chapter Four

Removing Barriers
to Student Learning

Melinda Eichhorn, Maria Marolda, Ellen Boiselle

PRE-READING REFLECTION

1. What are the reasons that students struggle in a class?
2. Why might students have difficulty in mathematics but less difficulty in other academic areas?
3. How do students' cognitive abilities, processing strategies, and problem-solving dispositions affect math learning?
4. How are you currently adapting your instruction to meet student needs?

WHAT TO EXPECT IN THIS CHAPTER

By understanding the varied cognitive and learning profiles that students bring to the classroom, teachers can anticipate the barriers that students experience in learning mathematics and can use that understanding to identify ways to mitigate challenges. Using a neuropsychological framework to understand the multiple factors that can either support or undermine student learning of mathematics, teachers and specialists can determine students' Mathematical Learning Profiles and, referring to them, make adaptations to the classroom environment and instructional strategies to promote students' success in mathematics and provide students with greater access to participation in the world of mathematics.

To understand and address student difficulties and vulnerabilities, teachers require professional-development opportunities and increased support in the classroom. Collaborative planning and problem-solving time with specialists in both mathematical and cognitive domains are critical. Mathematics educators and general educators must continue to review and rethink the emphases of a secondary mathematics curriculum.

In our increasingly technological society, quantitative literacy and facility in the fields of STEM are more important than ever. *Desirable difficulties* and engaging in productive struggle contribute to deep learning and are necessary for learning mathematics (Bjork, 1994; Lynch, Hunt, and Lewis, 2018). The degree to which students experience these difficulties must be carefully calibrated, lest they become so overwhelming that students are driven from the study of math. As we consider how administrators, principals, specialists, and teachers can inspire more students to take an interest in STEM courses and engage in productive struggle with mathematics, we must consider the barriers that they may have and are experiencing in classrooms.

There are various reasons why middle and high school students lose interest in math or take as few STEM courses as they can. Students may experience a mismatch between their inherent learning profiles and the demands of curricula and/or classroom expectations. This can constrain them from engaging meaningfully in mathematical activities and, thereby, create a barrier to learning.

Alternatively, negative experiences with mathematics during elementary school can result in low self-efficacy and diminished interest. Students may have a fixed mind-set and believe that they are not good at math because they were not born with the ability to *do math* (Dweck, 2006). Parents can exacerbate a fixed mind-set by saying that they were not *math people* in school and were never good at math either. Finally, students may not see the meaning and relevance of the math curriculum as it relates to their life's interests and goals.

How can we engage and support students by creating a learning environment that is supportive yet challenging so they can access rigorous mathematical content? How can we be flexible in meeting individual needs while attending to the whole class? Ultimately, how can we re-engage students who have given up on their math abilities?

LEARNER VARIABILITY

In considering learner variability, teachers often focus on the variation of innate intellectual potential or differences in levels of achievement. They should also consider variation in the features of students' overall cognitive profiles and inherent learning approaches. Each student has an individual profile of cognitive strengths and weaknesses; they bring this range of *abilities* to the classroom. Rose (2015) refers to this as a *jagged* learning profile, whereby each individual presents with a panoply of cognitive features, mind-sets, dispositions, and emotions that influence learning (p. 87).

Student Learning: A Neuropsychological Approach

In order to reduce barriers to student learning and to provide access to content, teachers must become familiar with the multiple cognitive and affective factors that influence learning. The more general cognitive construct and overarching framework from which we can view barriers to learning is the Child/World System (Holmes-Bernstein and Waber 1990; Waber, 2010). The Child/World System considers student learning differences as the dynamic interaction between what a child brings to a learning circumstance and what the learning circumstance demands of the child.

The key aspects of the Child/World System are the instances of *match* and *mismatch* of these two considerations. When features in a student's learning profile do not match the demands of the curriculum and the learning environment, the student is vulnerable to having difficulties in the classroom (Waber, 2010).

Using a Child/World System approach, a different view of a learning disability can be posited. See figures 4.1 and 4.2. A student's learning difficulties are seen as not residing in them as a "deficit" or "disability," but rather as a lack of "adaptation," the mismatch between what they bring to the classroom and what the world of the classroom expects of them (Lewis, 2014). Viewed from this perspective, the job of the teacher is not to "fix" a student's shortcomings but rather to adapt instruction to improve this interaction (Waber, 2010).

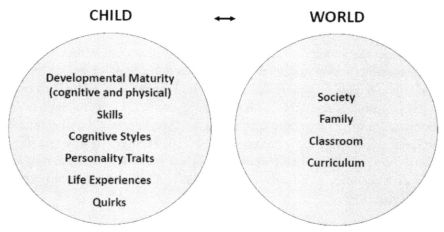

Figure 4.1.　Child/World System (Holmes-Bernstein and Waber, 1990; Waber, 2010)

THE "CHILD" IN THE CHILD/WORLD
SYSTEM FOR MATHEMATICS

The concept of a Child/World System as it relates to mathematics has been expanded by Marolda, Davidson, and Boiselle (Marolda and Davidson, 1994, 2000; Marolda and Boiselle, 2018a, 2018b). These authors argue that a focus on student learning in mathematics must move beyond a consideration of achievement per se to also include what students bring to the circumstance of mathematics in terms of inherent features of personal learning profiles that can influence effectiveness and what the world of mathematics asks of them.

According to a neuropsychological approach to mathematics learning, students bring a variety of reasoning skills, information-processing approaches, output skills, language skills, executive capacities, and affective postures to the learning of mathematics. Differences in the effectiveness or efficiency of the various components of a student's inherent "abilities" as they are called upon in the mathematical "world" in which the student functions can result in success or in great frustration in the mathematics classroom for both the teacher and student. See figure 4.2 following.

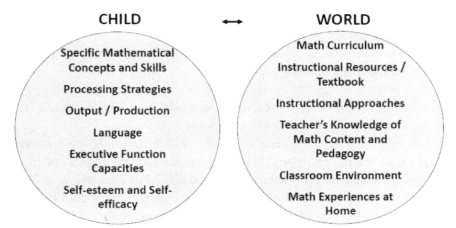

CHILD ⟷ **WORLD**

Specific Mathematical Concepts and Skills

Processing Strategies

Output / Production

Language

Executive Function Capacities

Self-esteem and Self-efficacy

Math Curriculum

Instructional Resources / Textbook

Instructional Approaches

Teacher's Knowledge of Math Content and Pedagogy

Classroom Environment

Math Experiences at Home

Figure 4.2. Child/World System for mathematics (Boiselle, 2018; Marolda and Davidson, 1994, 2000)

What students bring to the classroom may or may not be a good match for what the teacher or curriculum expects of them. Instances of mismatch may evoke feelings of anxiety or inadequacy and, in turn, a reluctance to engage in mathematics. As teachers understand and respond to student profiles, they can begin to break down barriers to learning mathematics by creating alternate avenues for learning that appeal to a student's inherent learning postures.

To be clear, breaking down barriers does not involve limiting challenge or watering down content. Rather, it involves reducing barriers, fostering meaningful engagement by offering varied approaches and meaningful contexts, and giving students access to the content (National Center on Universal Design for Learning, 2012).

MATHEMATICS LEARNING PROFILES

Marolda and Boiselle (2018a, 2018b) have expanded the view of "what a student brings to mathematics." They have defined the Mathematics Learning Profile (MLP) to include the level and reliability of discrete skills and understandings in mathematics, consideration of additional processing strategies, and an expanded view of executive function capacities.

As teachers seek to understand differences in students' MLP, they might consider the following questions:

- What are the preferred processing methods by which a student approaches or pursues a mathematical topic?
- How effective are the student's "output" skills? That is, how effectively can the student demonstrate what she has learned and understood?
- How effective are the student's "input skills"? For example, how do a student's language skills affect math learning? How well does the student deal with visual spatial demands in mathematics?
- How do the student's executive capacities (organizational skills, integration skills, working memory weaknesses, ability to sustain/shift between strategies and ability to handle increased load and complexity) affect personal learning and performance in mathematics?
- How do emotional, behavioral, or attentional factors influence math learning? See figure 4.3 below.

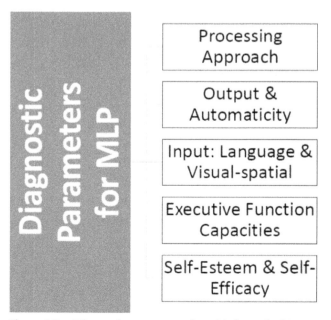

Figure 4.3. Diagnostic parameters for a Mathematical Learning Profile (Marolda and Boiselle, 2018a, 2018b)

Processing Approaches

Students approach or process mathematical information in three distinct ways: in a linear, global, or concrete fashion (Davidson, 1983; Marolda and Boiselle, 2018a, 2018b; Marolda and Davidson, 2000). Students who utilize a linear, "thinking up," approach to pursue mathematical situations proceed in a step-by-step, inductive fashion, focusing on individual details and steps, carefully implementing each and every step in turn. They often are described as "logical thinkers." Their reliance on careful, linear strategies, however, can sometimes occur at the expense of an appreciation of the underlying concepts or overarching frameworks to which individual elements contribute.

Students who prefer a global approach use "thinking down," deductive, strategies, where an initial focus is on overall frameworks or perspectives, with subsequent refinements applied in order to incorporate all detailed information and to achieve overall understanding and exact solutions. For a student using a global approach, a logical building-up approach may have little meaning unless it is framed within the context of overall thrust or goal. They are often referred to as "intuitive" thinkers. Students who favor intuitive conceptual approaches often resist paper-and-pencil approaches in favor of mental calculations. Moreover, exacting details and the need for precision may hold little relevance for global learners. They show little interest in exact solutions but are often content to just "be in the ballpark."

The concrete learner can eventually learn a concept or execute a procedure but typically requires concrete aids or relevant contexts to help organize and guide their efforts. Concrete learners often benefit from having arithmetic skills "anchored" in real-world problem situations in order to appreciate the practical meaning of procedure. Concrete learners like to "see," "touch," and "manipulate" materials as they work.

For example, they might prefer working with a math balance when learning about concepts of variable, equation, and equivalence. Although concrete strategies may be viewed by some teachers as time-intensive or primitive, these concrete materials and manipulations can provide important points of access for students who utilize a concrete processing approach. The challenge arises for concrete learners when they must work with higher-order, more abstract considerations when concrete models or relevant referents may be elusive.

Processing style is a critical component for understanding the secondary student, their learning and performance in the mathematics classroom, and their relationships to the mathematics curriculum. Instances of match or mismatch, between the way that a topic is presented and the way that the student processes information, can create barriers to student learning. Indeed, while many students can switch back and forth between deductive, inductive, and concrete strategies, others struggle to be flexible in their thinking. For these students, it is critical that they have access to the topic in their preferred processing mode so that meaningful foundations can be established and the students can experience success.

Strategies to Address Processing Issues

To remove barriers in the classroom, teachers should present different ways to access a given topic or skill, offering strategies that will appeal to different processing styles. If an approach is verbally driven, can it be presented in a conceptual or contextual way? Does the student need to be apprised of the "gist" of the topic before being able to execute associated procedures? Differentiated approaches to topics can be presented to all students in the classroom, with a request that each student try each strategy and then choose the option personally most comfortable. For students who struggle in math, however, the teacher may encourage a particular approach, lest the student become entangled and overwhelmed by different approaches.

Once a preferred approach has been identified, teachers should encourage the student to use that approach. Students who prefer a concrete processing strategy often need continued access to concrete materials or manipulatives while they are transitioning to an algorithm, rather than a short exposure to concrete materials at the introduction of the topic or skills. When designing instructional approaches for the concrete learner a teacher might consider how this topic or skill could be anchored with a real-world example and manipulatives.

Output Efficiency

Features such as pace and precision affect a student's performance in mathematics and the ability to readily demonstrate personal understanding (Boiselle, 2007, 2008; Marolda and Davidson, 2000). A student's output efficiency in mathematics is dependent upon respective pace, ability to maintain precision, and graphomotor output. While a student may understand a concept or procedure, output issues can undermine their efforts, creating a barrier to successful solutions and a source of frustration.

Fluency/Pace

In the teaching of mathematics, fluency with one-digit facts and with multidigit calculations receives a good amount of emphasis. Fluency is not only about speed and efficiency (ability to choose an appropriate, expedient strategy for a specific computation problem), but also accuracy (producing an accurate answer in a timely manner) and flexibility (ability to use number relationships with ease in computation) (Humphreys and Parker, 2015; Parrish, 2011; Russell, 2000). For some students, this emphasis on fluency comes at a cost.

When pressed to complete arithmetic examples quickly and efficiently, they can become anxious and frustrated; these emotions can effectively short-circuit their ability to demonstrate what they do understand. Some students will be able to self-correct their work when given extra time and the opportunity to do so, and other students may need encouragement, assistance to self-monitor, or strategies which will help them review and amend their solutions.

Precision

Students should aim to "calculate accurately and efficiently" and "express numerical answers with a degree of precision appropriate for the problem context" (Common Core State Standards Initiative, 2018, para. 7). When considering a student's challenges with precision in one-digit facts, a distinction should be made whether inaccuracy in one-digit facts occurs when the facts are called upon in isolation or whether they occur only in the context of executing procedures.

The former may reflect lack of automaticity or inefficient strategies while the latter would suggest that the students are challenged when required to incorporate multiple demands simultaneously. Students who are not exact with their calculations are often cited as being "careless" or "lazy."

Upon closer examination, however, a student might be using the correct approach, but have difficulty simultaneously maintaining precision with facts as they focus on the execution of the steps of a procedure. More experience practicing one-digit facts in isolation is unlikely to improve their efforts. For other students, imprecision may occur due to misreading operation signs, difficulties with visual perceptual skills, or difficulty shifting from one task to another.

For other students, imprecision may be secondary to their preferred global processing approaches, being students who adopt deductive strategies because they are more interested in the broader patterns and concepts than in the exactness of solutions. Difficulty with precision is rarely a matter of indifference, but it can be interpreted as such by teachers. Exploring the underlying reasons for imprecision is important.

Graphomotor Skills

Some students struggle with the actual act of writing, as a result of motor planning and/or fine motor issues. These students may try to avoid using paper and pencil when performing calculations because the act of writing itself is too laborious. Their written productions are often loosely formed or poorly controlled. At times they may not even be able not read their own writing. Because of their graphomotor challenges, they may attempt to juggle all of the calculations in their heads, which may exacerbate their struggles with precision and pace.

Strategies to Address Output Challenges

To determine the barriers a student may face, noticing the quality of the student's work is just as important as the accuracy or efficiency of the solutions (Waber, 2010). As teachers analyze students' errors and the process by which they obtain a solution, they should gather information about the student's pace, precision, and graphomotor skills. Students can grow to understand that their challenges in math may not indicate that they cannot learn math, but rather that they need to better demonstrate what, in fact, they have learned. With that understanding a barrier may be removed from their future efforts and promote success.

Students may face barriers in the math classroom because their pace, precision, and graphomotor skills do not match the teacher or classroom expectations. In order to break down barriers posed by output challenges, teachers can offer students additional time or limit the number of examples they must complete, with an emphasis on quality over quantity. As noted, students who struggle with output can become confrontational, defeated, or anxious. To avoid these counterproductive reactions, the teacher should take a deeper look at student work.

Is the student using the correct approach, but imprecision is getting in the way of obtaining a final accurate solution? If so, acknowledge that the student has used the correct approach, but must learn to monitor and revise personal answers. Students with graphomotor concerns may benefit from having the options to dictate their responses or to record their work using graph paper.

Providing multiple-choice formats, limiting copying demands, and providing a calculator to handle subroutines in the process of implementing longer strategies may prove helpful. For the teacher, separating output issues from learning issues helps to determine if a student requires re-instruction in a topic or the building of a strategy to improve the efficiency with which solutions are generated.

Input Efficiency: Facility with Language Demands in Mathematics

Expressive and receptive language skills play an important role in mathematics learning and performance, as these skills are necessary for both communication and mathematics reasoning, especially "word problems" (Witzel, Riccomini, and Herlong, 2013). Comprehending and expressing mathematics language can facilitate conceptual and procedural understanding (Hughes, Powell, and Stevens, 2016).

According to the Standards for Mathematical Practice, students who are proficient in mathematics must be able to "justify their conclusions, communicate them to others, and respond to the arguments of others" (Common Core State Standards Initiative, 2018, para. 4). While the standards mention that elementary students can use concrete and representational means to justify their reasoning, these options are not explicitly encouraged for use in the middle and upper grades.

Students with expressive language deficits may have difficulties with word retrieval, which can affect their ability to readily recall or generate mathematical terms (Marolda and Davidson, 1994, 2000). These students may also be vulnerable when they are asked to explain or justify their thinking. They may have more understanding of the concept than they can readily express in oral or written formats; this can affect their ability to engage in both small-group and whole-group discussions (Bryant, Kim, Hartman, and Bryant, 2006) and to justify their reasoning in written assignments on assignments, quizzes, and tests.

Students with receptive language challenges may struggle to understand instruction. These students often have difficulty making sense of word problems and may have difficulty following directions. The vocabulary of new concepts may be difficult for them to understand and follow as well. Sometimes students who struggle with receptive language may appear to have attention challenges, when in fact the inattention is secondary to challenges with understanding what has been presented or what is being asked (Marolda and Davidson, 2000).

Strategies to Address Language Issues in Mathematics

To address the needs of students with expressive language difficulties, particularly when students struggle with mathematical vocabulary used in the classroom, teachers can provide students with word banks to which they can refer. To mitigate difficulties in verbally explaining their thinking, teachers can offer students an opportunity to show their thinking through a diagram or other nonverbal model (Marolda and Boiselle, 2018a, 2018b; Marolda and Davidson, 2000).

To help students who are vulnerable with the receptive language demands of mathematics, teachers can offer repetitions and re-explanations—either in class or through posted videos that students can access after class. Teachers can be flexible in their methods for determining if a student understands a concept by allowing both verbal explanations and visual representations. Teachers might consider the following questions as they reflect on their practice: Did I provide both oral and written directions? Can the student retain and repeat back any of what was just said?

In a study by Butterworth (2005), students with math learning disabilities reported that they did not understand what the teacher was saying. The students said that they did not forget what the teacher said; rather, they did not understand it. Thus, at the end of an introduction of a topic, the teacher should check with a student to ensure the topic is fully understood.

Input Efficiency: Facility with Visual Spatial Cues

Math instruction relies on visual spatial skills, whether in the manipulatives that are being used or in the specific mathematical topics themselves. Geometry, measurement, and graphing are among the topics that call upon the appreciation of visual spatial patterns and relationships. When a student is having difficulty with abstract mathematical topics, it is often suggested that the topics be presented using visual supports or in a "multimodal fashion." However, students who are challenged by visual spatial demands are at risk for not benefiting from models dependent on visual spatial cues that are offered to support them.

Care must be taken in distinguishing cues that rely on visual spatial skills from cues that are merely concrete in nature. Concrete cues are direct in nature and do not rely on sophisticated perceptual skills or relationships. Counting chips, money, and fingers are all concrete cues. In contrast, models such as number line, circles (used as models for fractions), and geometric regions require the appreciation of overall spatial relationships.

Strategies to Address Visual Spatial Issues in Mathematics

To help students with visual spatial challenges, teachers must be keenly aware of topics with high visual spatial demands. For these students, curricular materials that place an emphasis on number lines should be carefully considered. In topics where visual spatial demands predominate, the teacher should add verbal interpretations of the topics or cues on which to focus, support important spatial considerations, and guide spatial manipulation of cues. When possible, visual spatial input should be simplified; for example, in formal geometry work, teachers might use transparencies or colored pencils to identify aspects of overlapping figures or software programs that help build and decompose geometric figures in a part-for-part manner.

Fortunately, in formal secondary geometry courses, much of the work is in terms of definitions of figures or logical proofs with less reliance on the interpretation of visual spatial relationships and more reliance on verbalization and logical thinking. Thus, while the traditional geometry course may be challenging to those with visual spatial issues, these weaknesses do not necessarily preclude access to formal geometric work if the demand to interpret the visual cues is simplified.

Executive Function Capacities

Students' executive processes are an important component of their MLP (Marolda and Boiselle, 2018a, 2018b). Just as executives manage their workers, executive function capacities help a student to manage and coordinate personal processing and thinking skills. Executive functions are regulatory or managerial cognitive abilities that allow an individual to initiate behavior; inhibit undesirable behavior or distractions; plan, organize, integrate, and shift between strategies when necessary; and monitor and evaluate the effectiveness of one's behaviors and problem-solving abilities (CAST, 2018; Meltzer, 2010).

Executive function capacities that have a particular impact on mathematics learning and performance include organizational skills, working memory skills, integration skills, and ability to deal with increased information load and complexity (Geary, Hoard, Nugent, and Byrd-Craven, 2007; Marolda and Boiselle, 2018a, 2018b; Meltzer, 2010).

Organizational Skills

Organizational skills in math range from students' abilities to pursue their calculations on paper to organizing a strategy with which to attempt a word problem or to bring together the elements of two-dimensional geometric configurations. Students with organizational problems may have difficulty aligning numerals on the page, which can lead to calculation errors with place values (Marolda and Boiselle, 2018a, 2018b; Marolda and Davidson, 2000).

They may also struggle with following through on initial approach to a given example or problem—initiating a correct first step but struggling to extend their strategy to its conclusion. Some students are able to pick up organizational strategies by observing how adults proceed, while other students require explicit instruction and must have the steps broken down for them into manageable parts.

Working Memory Skills

Working memory is "the ability to hold a mental representation of information in mind while simultaneously engaged in other mental processes"

(Geary et al., 2007, p. 88; Geary, 2013). Working memory involves the student's ability to temporarily store information, while using that information to calculate or make decisions about the next steps (Schuchardt, Maehler, and Hasselhorn, 2008). Students who struggle with working memory can sometimes lose the overall goal in problem-solving situations or when implementing multistep procedures or strategies, becoming entangled with the elements or steps involved (Marolda and Boiselle, 2018a, 2018b).

Students with auditory working memory difficulties can struggle following instructions, even short instructions. These students often mention that they forgot what to do or what they were instructed to do (Baddeley, 2007). They tend to lose the goal to which they are directed as they work through the individual steps to reach that goal.

It is important to determine whether a student has memory difficulties because the original information was never encoded or understood or if the student is having difficulty accessing the information when they need it (Marolda and Davidson, 2000). If the original information was not understood, re-teaching will be required with a change in the instructional approach to one that is more closely aligned with the student's processing style.

Integration Skills

For students to manage multiple demands or subroutines within a problem or to derive meaning from novel or complex information, they use a cognitive process referred to as "integration" (Waber, 2010). In mathematics, the demand for integration skills become more prominent in the middle and upper schools, where the emphasis shifts from developing a discrete skill to merging multiple skills to achieve a solution (Marolda and Boiselle, 2018a, 2018b).

For example, in the upper elementary and middle school grades, demands for integration are manifest: in the need to maintain precision in one-digit facts as calculation procedures are pursued; in executing the traditional "long division" algorithm, which shifts from "estimate, multiply, subtract, bring down"; and in fraction topics, where students must manage multiple considerations when considering non-unit fractions and when performing operations on fractions. Integration skills are critical to application problems, as a student needs to identify the salient information and integrate how the details fit with the "big picture." The student then must both plan an approach and calculate a solution.

More generally, students with integration problems typically become overwhelmed by tasks that require multiple steps and may have difficulty determining which information is relevant. They may be able to handle a concept or procedure at initial levels but then have difficulty as the numbers involved become bigger or as the concept is extended to abstract levels (Marolda and Boiselle, 2018a, 2018b). When faced with novelty or complexity, students may feel completely lost and not be able to mount an effective strategy. Limited integration skills have a debilitating impact and constitute a significant barrier to learning mathematics.

Ability to Deal with Increased Load and Complexity

By their very nature, middle school and secondary school curricula are marked by increased load and complexity. While overall cognitive potential is a factor influencing whether students can handle these challenges, it is also true that students with organizational, integration, and working memory weaknesses are at significant risk under those demands. The constellation of these challenges can have an overwhelming effect in specific topics or courses at the middle and secondary school levels.

Strategies to Address Executive Function Capacities Challenges

For students who struggle with organizational skills, the elements of topics or steps of procedures should be carefully highlighted and the "linkage" between them emphasized. Students can be supported with "flow charts," which guide their approaches, or by the use of a Mathematical Notebook, where a topic is described in terms of a specific example and the steps for tracking the path to a solution are described in succinct dialogue boxes. The emphasis in providing such supports is the nurturing of fading dependence on them, until students can pursue strategies or steps of procedures on their own.

For students with working memory weaknesses, teachers should present information carefully, in small increments, to ensure that the student incorporates all the salient elements. Paper and pencil formats should be encouraged, recording each aspect or step of a procedure in turn, thereby minimizing the amount of information the student must hold in memory while pursuing a procedure or strategy. Moreover, the demand for mental calculation should be minimized in favor of written approaches.

For students having difficulties with integration skills and subsequent difficulties with load and complexity, the building of strategies should be emphasized as much as the building of specific math skills. Students with integration challenges require explicit structures to guide their efforts. Direct instruction and supervised rehearsal of metacognitive skills is critically important. Metacognition is the ability to develop strategies for planning an approach to tasks, for organizing the steps of a task to achieve a solution, and for monitoring the results.

The goal in teaching these strategies is that the student comes to understand why, when, and how a strategy is used. Students should then be taught to use these metacognitive strategies thoughtfully, rather than in a rote and ritualistic manner (Marolda and Boiselle, 2018a, 2018b). Part of metacognition is self-monitoring or questioning and evaluating one's approach (Bouck and Bouck, 2016; Montague, 2007). Explicit instruction, with direct modeling, cuing, and feedback, in self-monitoring, helps students to think, plan, and apply their strategies independently, and to evaluate their understanding (Montague, 2005; Witzel and Little, 2016).

Montague (2007) argued for teaching a combination of cognitive and metacognitive processes to students who struggle with problem solving (Montague and Dietz, 2009). Students need cognitive skills to analyze and paraphrase application problems, which is a comprehension strategy, as well as to visualize what the problem is asking (Montague, 2005; Montague and Dietz, 2009). They also need metacognitive skills as they self-verbalize, self-question, and self-evaluate (Montague, 2005).

Consider using "think alouds," or process modeling, to demonstrate for students how to use the cognitive and metacognitive strategies in a classroom (Dougherty, Bryant, Bryant, and Shin, 2016; IRIS Center, 2013, Montague, 2005). Perhaps list the strategies on a cue sheet, so students can refer to them in math class and during homework. As students gain confidence and internalize the strategies, their need for the cue sheet will diminish.

For secondary students who are challenged by increased load and complexity, the choice of courses is critical. Instruction should be offered in courses where fundamental aspects of a topic, rather than the most sophisticated intricacies, are developed. In settings where concepts are explicit, where there is a moderated pace of instruction, and where output demands are moderated, instrumentation is critical.

Self-Esteem and Self-Efficacy

Students come to our classrooms with various beliefs about their math abilities, which can affect their performance. Students in middle school and high school math classrooms often hold firm beliefs about their math abilities. Some have experienced great success in their past mathematics classrooms, resulting in confidence. Others, however, many have experienced extreme frustration. These students tend be hesitant in their responses and have various degrees of confidence in their abilities. These students also tend to have a negative, fixed mathematical mind-set and can be anxious about making mathematical mistakes (Dweck, 2006).

It is most important that a student remain available to math learning, with a willingness to engage in instruction and not to resist or be fearful of topics that might be new or initially challenging. Limited self-esteem, and the resultant reduction of self-efficacy caused by frustration and anxiety, can serve as powerful barriers to learning mathematics at the secondary school level.

Strategies to Address Diminished Self-Esteem and Self-Efficacy

Students with limited self-esteem and self-efficacy regarding mathematics require encouragement and supportive monitoring, having their teacher check on their progress as they work toward a solution. At the beginning of the year, teachers can ask students to complete a self-assessment about mathematics and their past experiences in math.

With this information, teachers, students, and specialists can conference together to discuss the various aspects of the students' feelings toward mathematics, to clarify their struggles in mathematics, and to brainstorm together as to how they can overcome challenges. It is equally important to query students about those areas of mathematics with which they feel comfortable or that they find enjoyable. If students better understand their strengths and difficulties, they can set goals and self-advocate for what they know they require to succeed in the math classroom.

To bolster student efforts, responses should be "judged" or graded on more than the final solutions generated. For example, if the emphasis of the assessment is determining the student's problem-solving strategies, questions posed might be, for example, "what is your first step?"; partial credit can be given for those portions of the solution process that are correct.

Furthermore, the level of difficulty or of examples on a given test or assignment can be "leveled," giving simpler examples with which students can be successful, and then building forward to more complex items. Varying the levels of difficulty of examples presented allows students to see if they, in fact, do have a basic understanding, but they have difficulty as demands increase. More generally, teachers can address diminished or eroded self-esteem by providing opportunities for orchestrated successes, recognizing and highlighting successes achieved.

THE "WORLD" IN THE CHILD/WORLD SYSTEM OF MATHEMATICS

Although students bring a variety of abilities and approaches to the learning of mathematics, as manifest in their MLP, the demands of the mathematics to be "learned" must be considered. In the mathematics classroom, students face a variety of demands that are not of their own making: the curriculum, the teacher's instructional style, and the classroom environment itself. In some cases these demands are a "good" match with the features of a student's inherent MLP; for other students there is a "mismatch," which leaves them vulnerable to frustration and even failure.

RELEVANCE OF THE MATHEMATICS CURRICULUM

At the secondary level, students must know the relevance of mathematics to their present and future lives. A common complaint at the secondary level is "How am I going to use this?" Framing topics, skills, and assignments within a context that is relevant, valuable, and meaningful to students will allow teachers to engage and sustain student interest (CAST, 2018).

Strategies to Address the Issue of the Relevance of the Curriculum

Nationally, many mathematicians and mathematics educators, at both college and secondary levels, are critically evaluating the current secondary mathematics curriculum for its relevance to students as well as to the future worlds that students will be expected to navigate. In the meantime, in order to embed meaning and relevance into the mathematics classroom, teachers can collaborate with colleagues who teach other subjects to integrate units where possible across departments.

Although such collaboration between math and science departments seems an immediate choice, the use of mathematics in social studies warrants particular investigation. The inclusion of engineering in STEM initiatives is another encouraging sign. Administrators should encourage teachers to engage in collaborative planning with colleagues in other subject areas to consider ways that the curricula could be integrated, as this will emphasize the real-world applications of mathematics.

At the middle school level, programs have been developed to foster this "integrated approach to learning," including *The Voyage of the* Mimi, (which aired on PBS in the 1980s) and Project CALC ("Calculus As a Laboratory Course") at Duke University. Some alternative high schools are also experimenting with nontraditional curriculum approaches. Teachers should be encouraged to visit schools where alternate approaches are being implemented. Teachers can utilize resources in the outside community, with field trips, short-term internships during vacations, and guest speakers to emphasize the links between "school mathematics" and "mathematics in the real world."

Classroom Contexts: Teachers and Learning Environments

According to Hilyard (2013), students who participate in class have a connection with and trust in their teacher. Trust can be built over time between mathematics educators and students through belief in students' ability, care for students, and the competence of the instructor (Hilyard,

2013). As teachers anticipate having diverse individuals in their class-rooms and become more sensitive in planning their lessons and assignments with diversity of approach in mind, students may, in turn, develop more trust in the teacher, particularly as they come to recognize that the teachers are trying to reach them in terms that are compatible with their inherent learning approaches in order to help them become effective mathematics students.

Strategies to Address Learning Environments

Teachers can develop welcoming learning environments by providing students with clear expectations so that students know what success looks and sounds like in their mathematical work and small-group discussions (Eichhorn, DiMauro, Lacson, and Dennie, 2019). Teachers can also emphasize to students that their errors or confusions are just as important as their solutions (Ma, 2010). Valuing mistakes and using them as learning tools enhance students' sense of worth and contribution to the learning process. By moderating and modifying demands, teachers can communicate their belief that any student can be successful at some level in personal mathematical efforts.

Incorporating Resources from Outside the Classroom

A typical resource for the teacher of a struggling math student is standardized testing, which likely has been undertaken to determine the source of the student's academic challenges. Traditional assessments and standardized tests, however, are unlikely to yield the rich qualitative data helpful in understanding why students are having difficulties in math or the barriers they may be experiencing in the classroom. Formal techniques, particularly standardized tests in mathematics, should be used judiciously and complemented by additional information about how a student is processing information.

As designed, most current standardized tests report deficits: "the what" of a student's difficulties not "the why." The "why" of a student's errors might be revealed by a student's work product. The work product of the student, both classwork and worksheets used during standardized tests, should be evaluated to determine where the student went awry. A more robust way to determine the "why" is to call upon a math coach or special educator.

A teacher should collaborate with and rely on the math coach or special educator to provide more individualized attention to students who are facing challenges. These specialists can gather important information about a student's mathematical learning profile using informal and formal assessment techniques. When possible, a clinical interview might be used, sometimes referred to as a diagnostic interview, originally developed by Jean Piaget (Ginsburg, 1997). Alternatively, the coach or special educator can sit with the student as the student engages in the written portion of standardized tests to observe and query how the student is proceeding or where the student struggles.

For encouragement. newer and alternative assessment techniques that use a process-oriented approach are now being developed by mathematics educators (Burns, 2012; Marolda, Davidson, and Boiselle, 2015). These assessments may provide guidelines and offer adaptations to traditional assessment approaches. They include a wider range of mathematical topics and highlight the approaches and qualitative features of a student's efforts in mathematics (Boiselle, 2007, 2008).

The Role of Principals and Administrators

Principals and administrators play an important role in helping teachers and specialists as they seek to identify and address the barriers to math learning. Administrators can encourage collaboration among general educators, math specialists, coaches, and special educators that is necessary to help students maintain and generalize strategies to solve mathematical problems (Montague, 2006). Providing in-class support and planning time with specialists is vital to allowing math teachers to dig deeper and uncover student understanding and misconceptions.

Principals and administrators can provide supported time to complete a "math child study" in which educators confer about a student, consider a learning profile, review previous cognitive testing (if available), and suggest strategies. For example, once the teacher or specialist has gathered both qualitative and quantitative data, a collaborative meeting can be helpful to analyze the results and gain multiple perspectives. The team may determine that additional information is needed; perhaps another interview will need to be completed, or follow-up observations of the student be conducted to gather additional insights.

Once teachers begin to implement adapted instruction to address barriers to learning, they will continue to need collaborative dialogue to judge and amend those adaptations as necessary. Principals and administrators should support and encourage teachers to engage in professional-development activities outside the school, both in terms of instructional strategies and curriculum review. Short-term sabbaticals in the workplace might also be considered as opportunities for teachers to "get in touch with the real world."

SUMMARY

As school teams attempt to develop student interest in mathematics and STEM courses, it is essential to consider why a student might be vulnerable in the secondary mathematics classroom and may have lost interest in mathematics. Student learning and performance are affected by the interaction of the features of their MLP and the "world" of mathematics in which they operate. What students bring to the classroom may or may not be aligned with the instructional approaches of the classroom, or what the teacher or the curriculum expects of students, and this may account for some of the resistance or anxiety students feel toward learning mathematics.

The students' feelings of self-efficacy and self-esteem in mathematics are equally important. They may come to the secondary level with "baggage" that limits their ability to be fully engaged in mathematics instruction and appreciative of the beauty of mathematics. For all students, teachers must present information in formats that simultaneously engage student interest and provide for carefully orchestrated experiences of success. Moreover, the curriculum and the presentation of topics should be carefully considered with references to relevant contexts and meaningful applications.

A teacher will likely have students with a variety of MLP in a classroom. Although the teacher in the classroom often cannot tailor each lesson to an individual student's profile, knowledge of the variety of barriers that students can experience in the mathematics classroom can provide a framework for shaping mathematical content and instructional strategies by offering differentiated approaches and meaningful context. Collaborative planning time and in-class support are vital for teachers to begin this approach.

As teachers and specialists take steps to understand the MLP of their students, they can anticipate the barriers and implement strategies to help students internalize strategies and overcome or remove barriers. By embedding math instruction in meaningful and relevant contexts, teachers will likely ignite or reignite students' interest in mathematics.

When teachers and specialists aim to adjust their instructional approaches and learning environments in the mathematics classroom, students will experience fewer barriers to learning math. Interest in providing opportunities to align the "child" and "the world of mathematics" will result in a more meaningful and robust mathematical experience that will likely foster greater interest and participation in the domain of mathematics as well as the related areas of science, engineering, and technology.

Chapter Five

Engaging Students by Flipping the Classroom

Jill B. Branyon

PRE-READING REFLECTION

1. How can principals lead a paradigm shift and change in school culture for teaching mathematics?
2. What strategies can principals use to create a teacher buy-in to change?
3. What supports must principals provide teachers who are creating a mind-shift to teaching mathematics?
4. What can principals expect in terms of teacher efficacy, student performance, and school culture when paradigm shifts occur?

WHAT TO EXPECT IN THIS CHAPTER

When principals and school leaders engage in collaboration with teachers and students, the results can be astounding. By identifying the obstacles that particular students have in their learning process and applying sound research and best practices, teachers can create a paradigm shift in their own practices that lead to greater satisfaction in their work and improvement in student learning. Principals who lead in these changes can expect improved results including student gains in learning, decreased dropout rates and discipline referrals, increased teacher collaboration and efficacy, better student and teacher morale, and greater teacher retention.

THE CHALLENGE OF CHANGE

Principals who are able to ask the big questions can expect resistance to change, but with collaborative approaches can move forward and lead faculty to see the need for a paradigm shift. Teachers come on board when changes benefit them. Teachers come on board when they are valued and included in the questions that need to be addressed.

Regardless of the approach taken, such as flipping the classroom, creating interactive learning opportunities, or through lesson studies and increased rigor and STEM lessons, teachers can find ways to meet student-learning needs, increase their own satisfaction, and boost school morale. The complete makeover begins with the leadership and builds with collaborative approaches to identifying the true needs of the student community, admitting that what is being done is not working, and taking a risk to try new ways of teaching and learning.

Principals who lead in risk-taking create an atmosphere of innovative practice. Even when the resources are not available, schools that use collaboration and best practices can find a way to meet students where they are and move them toward success. The specific stories of Clintondale High School and Cochrane Collegiate Academy present a clear picture of what can be accomplished when a paradigm shift occurs and principals are willing to ask the important questions.

Principals and administrators, like teachers, must demonstrate that students are learning by using test data, graduation rates, and attendance. When the evidence is lacking or tells a different story, principals and teachers must explore possible solutions. Research shows that when principals lead and teachers collaborate on problem solving, then student learning increases (Goddard, Miller, Larson, and Goddard, 2010). When mathematics teachers collaborate to solve problems, their efficacy increases and students learn at deeper levels (*Common Core Mathematics in PLC at Work*, 2012; Protheroe, 2008). Demonstrating how principal leadership and teacher collaboration produce results are examples that illustrate the point.

According to Greg Green (personal interview, August 10, 2018), principals who explore answers to meeting student needs in a shared format with teachers find several obstacles. In 2010, Clintondale High School, Clinton Township, Michigan, found that freshmen were failing at alarming rates, including 44 percent in mathematics. The students lacked motivation and engagement. The school was 85 percent minority, and the school culture lacked pride and hope. The principal faced teachers who were not interested in change in addition to tight financial constraints, a lack of technology, and a strong teachers' union.

When Green invited his faculty to consider why students were failing and falling through the cracks, he considered an idea from when he coached softball as the possibility (Clintondale, 2013). As Green began to explore how courses were taught and students engaged, he found that teachers were intimidated by observation and being videoed. He found that the study of class instruction that the teachers were doing most of the talking and students were just sitting and listening. As Green began to introduce one option, a flipped classroom, he began the process by promoting the advantages for the teachers.

Green's approach to introducing the flipped classroom focused mainly on the benefits to teachers. He found three very distinct responses: some teachers were wholeheartedly involved; others were in a wait-and-see pattern; and others refused to budge. Taking risks for the sake of student outcomes comes with a variety of pushbacks as well as pats on the back from teachers. Thinking outside the box brings conflict as well as rewards.

RESULTS

Clintondale High School in Michigan decided to flip the classroom as part of their best practice agenda of 80/20. Students should be working in class 80 percent of the time; teachers should be presenting instructions or information only 20 percent of the time. In the initial class studies, class time showed 99 percent teacher instruction and 1 percent student engagement. Reviewing such practices required lesson studies across the school and teacher collaboration. Green (2018) employed a selling tactic called 14/5. To introduce this change in instruction, he would mention it 14 times; the last 5 times would come from other teachers who were finding success and students who were demanding that all teachers change so they could learn.

Green commented that thinking like a salesperson helped his cause and he focused entirely on the advantages to teachers. He assured teachers that this move toward 80/20 would give them greater control over their students and student performance and would lighten their workload approximately 60 percent. He declared that teachers were ready to try this new approach based on the advantages to their own lives.

He assured teachers that they would be in control throughout the changeover and find even greater academic freedom in the process. Green faced difficult obstacles including having no budget for technology and having almost no technology already available at Clintondale. By focusing on simple technologies with which people were familiar and were without cost and by assuring teachers that the changes would be beneficial to themselves, Green was able to move forward. Green remarked that the tool was the least of the issues. He focused on teacher benefits, knowing full well that their buy-in would lead to better learning for students.

The results were phenomenal. In data collected at the beginning (2010) and again in 2011, a number of significant results occurred. First, the ninth grade failure rate in mathematics was reduced from 44 percent to 13 percent, a reduction of 31 percent. In a single year, ninth grade discipline incidents fell from 736 in 2010, to 249 in 2011, and even further to 187 in 2012. Green attributed the reduction to students finding greater success in the classroom and learning in ways that met their needs. School-wide failures dropped from 35 percent to 9 percent in a two-year period from 2010 to 2012.

The growth in student performance on the ACT in 2013 and again in 2016 was more than double the national average for gains (https://www.pbs.org/newshour/education/what-does-a-flipped-classroom-look-like-2). The percentage of improvement for eleventh graders, 2012–2015, was from 66 percent gains in two years to a high of 77 percent gains in mathematics. Teachers were buying in, streamlining their teaching using digital technology and using class time to work with students one-on-one.

The results were impressive. Graduation rates began to climb from 80 percent in 2011 to 97 percent in 2015, a gain of 17 percent in graduates. College attendance also rose after the flipped-classroom approach began from 63 percent to 81 percent over the same time frame. In every statistic that measured student success, the results have been significant and have continued to improve.

Green cautioned that just flipping the classroom accomplished very little; when teachers had control over independent practice and homework by students working during the school day, the gains became significant. Teachers began slowly creating videos for students using the available technology. They moved from lecture instruction to using video technology and learned to use class time in efficient ways that support student learning and collaboration. How the teachers engaged students in the classroom and utilized the class time was pivotal and created a paradigm shift. Teachers began to see students as learners and creators of their own knowledge, and the results were astounding.

Ten years later, Green has a new role as superintendent of Clinton Township School District. The district continues to insist on 80/20 in a district that is highly impoverished and more than 85 percent minority students. The entire culture of the school changed and led to a student attendance rate of approximately 95 percent as well as a nearly 97 percent graduation rate. The changes for teachers led to a transformation in school culture that is collaborative and collegial, reducing teacher attrition and bringing teachers more satisfaction in teaching.

Teachers expressed that having control over the work students carry out in the classroom has led to significant improvement for students. The support that students now receive from their teachers increases student understanding and confidence. As evidenced by the significant gains in important areas, the decision to use best practice with technology has met the needs of students. The grassroots effect of flipping the classroom has worked well with the demographic and needs of the Clinton Township School District.

A wide variety of packaged programs and approaches marketed to schools and school districts often tout phenomenal results using a specific tool. But without teacher buy-in and collaborative decision-making, the results are short-lived. Sustained student growth relates directly to teacher participation, teacher benefits, and teacher beliefs regarding classroom procedures.

School administrators often wade through the myriad of options, looking for a magic bullet to save the day. The research shows that a number of innovations achieve the desired results, but that implementation depends on principal-teacher collaboration, teacher input and ideas, student-teacher collaboration, and creating a new school culture of grit and responsibility. In essence, a paradigm shift occurs and leads the entire culture and school to change.

The improvement in mathematics education requires that principals invest time, leadership, and resources in the process (*Common Core*

Mathematics in PLC at Work, 2012; Protheroe, 2008). Principals who take this leadership role will see a variety of results in their schools (Goddard, Miller, Larson, and Goddard, 2010). The school culture shifts to a student focus, a more positive approach to teaching arises and a collaborative atmosphere emerges. While some districts and educational products promoters tout amazing results from a top-down approach, the evidence points to more engagement and collaborations from teachers in the building leading to long-term improvement and results.

SIMILAR REPORT FROM DIFFERENT SCHOOLS

The same focus is occurring in other countries. One school in Japan made significant progress in redefining the academic reputation of the school through significant collaboration between the principal and teachers. While the principal was a history teacher before taking the leadership mantle, he found ways to collaborate with the mathematics department, providing them extensive together time. With a focus on engaging students of all ability levels, he helped mathematics teachers collaborate by providing time release to design and implement new approaches to teaching geared at student engagement and high expectations for all students.

Only half the students in this school had a STEM focus, with the rest having more of a social arts focus. However, those who focused in STEM were all expected to gain conceptual understanding. Their standardized tests scores attest to their success.

The shift toward a change based on individual school and student needs, plus teacher professional development, support, and options to collaborate pay the greatest dividends in terms of student confidence, engagement, and results. Once the eighth lowest-performing middle school in its state, Cochrane Collegiate Academy reversed course and is swiftly raising student achievement by investing in research-based teaching strategies and building teacher collaboration through professional development (Edutopia, 2011).

Former middle school administrator Joshua Bishop explained that students were failing and the school was failing in a variety of ways including discipline, attendance, and academic performance (Edutopia, 2011). Poverty and low teacher morale were among factors that contributed to the school's failure. Shana Oliver, the instructional facilitator, remarked in an interview that, "there was a lot of teacher turnover back then and I think we were in a mentality where it was just about teachers surviving" (Edutopia, 2011).

A math teacher in the school said that what she witnessed when she arrived was mayhem: children just running up and down the halls, hollering and screaming. A first-year teacher left because morale was so low (Edutopia, 2011). Once the administration and faculty researched a variety of instructional approaches to teaching based on lesson studies and teacher instruction versus student engagement, they chose an interactive approach.

Oliver explained to Edutopia (2011), "when we began to look at what we were doing in the classroom and why our kids weren't getting it. And we found the root of that to be the way that we were teaching our students." The faculty and administration committed themselves to professional development of more than ninety hours to transform teaching from a delivery system of information into an interactive student-focused approach (Edutopia, 2011). The instructional facilitator explained the nonnegotiables that all faculty employed.

These included an essential question and vocabulary that focused the lesson, an activating strategy to draw students into the lesson by relating to their experiences, limited lecture, and graphic organizers to help students learn how to organize information. Students had to do and say from beginning to end, showing teacher-student collaboration and student-student collaboration. In the professional-development meetings, Oliver modeled every part of the nonnegotiables with other teachers, who then implemented them in their classes. A paradigm shift occurred in all the classrooms, but the results in the mathematics classes were astounding. The focus was no longer on teaching mathematics, but rather on students learning mathematics utilizing an interactive approach.

Cochrane experienced increased teacher collaboration and better morale. Students performed at higher levels, more than doubling their percentage on grade level; attendance increased and is still at high levels in 2018 according to the new principal; and student discipline referrals decreased. While Cochrane has become a magnet school, the focus is still on student learning. According to Principal Goldberg (personal correspondence, August 11, 2018), teacher collaboration is one key to success.

Students continue to struggle with academic performance demands; but Cochrane ranked 56th out of 2,557 high schools in North Carolina. Through innovative practice, focused professional development, lesson studies, and teacher collaboration, Cochrane has found ways to engage students in learning, improve teacher morale, improve attendance, and reduce discipline referrals. The educators' paradigm shift was to focus on ways that their students learn best.

Principals can expect a paradigm shift and change in school culture. Teachers and students begin to take ownership of student learning. A shift from lesson observations (how well the teacher performs) toward a lesson study (which focuses on students and how deeply they were challenged and engaged in the learning) becomes necessary for long-term results as evidenced in the examples of Clintondale High School and Cochrane Collegiate Academy.

In Scotland, mathematics faculty designed joint lessons that numerous teachers developed, assessed, and modified. When teachers move away from their own teaching performance to student performance, a paradigm shift occurs. Among other paradigm shifts, teachers become reflective in their work, use data to track the engagement of students, and seek research to inform practice. Focus is on how well students are learning and developing as mathematicians rather than who is passing tests, paying attention in class, or showing effort. At the model school in Scotland teacher collaboration resulted in their students scoring in the upper 20 percent in the country on standardized tests.

Teachers begin to focus on what they can change, such as content and instruction. They look for more technology, real-life problems, and open-ended engagement in mathematics (Clintondale, 2013; Cochrane, 2018). Teachers exchange efficient performance of procedural learning for deeper contextual leaning and mathematical investigations.

Teacher collaboration in Japan was not just confined to the local school. Teachers visited other schools as collaboration became the norm. Teachers are able to engage students in discourse and to open up investigations that truly interest learners. Cultural changes in the mathematics classroom do not occur overnight, but require intentional support and guidance from school administrators. Teachers become student-focused when building leaders become teacher-focused. Just as students must be trusted with their own learning and their own questions, teachers must be trusted to pursue best practices.

As the school moves forward in innovative practices such as flipped classrooms, interactive learning, and real-world approaches to learning mathematics with a STEM focus, teachers experience increased teacher efficacy. Teacher efficacy is the belief that teachers make a real difference in the lives and performance of students.

Teacher efficacy motivates teachers to keep researching and keep trying until every student is successful. Teacher efficacy is a simple idea with significant implications. Teacher efficacy is a personal evaluation by teachers of their own capabilities to create student engagement and learning, even among those students who may not be successful or engaged (Protheroe, 2008). School leaders must help build teacher efficacy in the school. In the same way that student grit creates successful students, then, teacher efficacy creates successful teachers. School administrators who find ways to create an atmosphere of *making a difference* in the classroom create teacher efficacy.

SUMMARY

The more teachers collaborate the more excited they become about impacting their students' learning. Schools in Scotland, Japan, and South Korea that had a collaboration focus generated real student excitement and provided a positive learning atmosphere. Principals hold the key to improved mathematics scores by providing time and support for teachers. The resulting collaboration impacts the entire school's culture and results, as evidenced by Clintondale High School and Cochrane Collegiate Academy.

Chapter Six

Student-Centered Learning with Productive Struggle

Lauren Sager

PRE-READING REFLECTION

1. How might students be asked to struggle with mathematics concepts in the classroom?
2. When students are actively learning through student-centered activities, how does the role of the teacher change?
3. Have you been in a classroom where student-centered activities are emphasized? How has that changed the interactions within the classroom?

WHAT TO EXPECT IN THIS CHAPTER

The reader will learn what is meant by productive struggle and student-centered learning and how they can be implemented in the mathematics classroom. With an emphasis on student-centered learning, the role of teacher and student change. Teachers are required to put more work into task selection and their responses to students' inquiries. Students need to share their knowledge, ask questions, and generally grapple with the material. This chapter focuses on available resources for teachers to use collaboratively on the journey to creating more student-centered learning in the classroom. The reader will understand the advantages of utilizing NCTM materials and applying them in a classroom setting.

HOW DOES A TEACHER UTILIZE
PRODUCTIVE STRUGGLE?

The call for a change in mathematics teaching is not new, nor is it unique. Professional organizations such as the National Council of Teachers of Mathematics (NCTM) have presented the case for change numerous times, and government policies such as No Child Left Behind and the Common Core have tried to legislate change. Chapter 1 of this book discusses some of narrative of this change.

One of the major narratives of the call for change has been a focus on productive struggle. Teaching methods that emphasize productive struggle are described as embracing "a view of students' struggles as opportunities for delving more deeply into understanding the mathematical structure of problems and relationships among mathematical ideas, instead of simply seeking correct solutions" (NCTM, 2014, p. 48). The line between productive struggle and unproductive struggle is a fine one, and struggle where students are not able to make any progress tends to leave learners and teachers frustrated. Therefore, this is not a simple concept to implement in the classroom.

While not groundbreaking methodology, most teachers have not experienced productive struggle as students. Traditionally, mathematics courses are taught by a teacher who is the authority in the classroom and who often exemplifies the role of dispersing knowledge for students to memorize. Research shows that teachers tend to teach as they were taught. It involves much more time, effort, and a much higher risk of failure for a teacher to teach in an entirely new way. Because most current teachers experienced their own education in classrooms where procedural rather than conceptual learning was emphasized, the opposition to change can be strong. Moving to teaching with an entirely new set of goals requires a significant amount of risk and time.

In a classroom where students are asked to productively struggle with the material, the teacher is no longer the centerpiece of the classroom but the guide. Knowledge is not disseminated to the students, it is created by the students. They are asked to grapple with difficult problems and sometimes discover the material for themselves. The teacher is not considered the sole authority, but rather a resource.

As guides, teachers must change their own way of thinking. Their role is not to give the answers to students, but to help them arrive at the answer themselves. The biggest challenge for teachers who are trying to ask their students to engage in productive struggle is how to provide support, while not removing the challenge from the task at hand. Included in this major shift in the role of the teacher is trying to keep students thinking at a high level while giving students the support they need to keep them from reaching the point of unproductive struggle. The teacher has the difficult job of breaking down the problem enough for the students so that they can make progress, while not making the answer trivial or an exercise in fact recall.

Many mathematics education researchers have researched and described task selection. Smith and Stein (2011) break down task selection into two main categories: lower-level demands and higher-level demands. Lower-level demands include tasks that involve memorization, or procedures without connections, while higher-level demands include procedures with connections, and "doing mathematics" (Smith and Stein, 2011, p. 16). Lower-level tasks are those which are either unambiguous fact recall or are algorithmic with little to no ambiguity about how to arrive at the correct answer or what it is. These tasks also have no connection to the concepts that underlie the procedure or recalled fact and emphasize a single correct answer.

On the other hand, higher-level demands come from tasks that have connections with deeper levels of mathematical thinking and concepts. They may be procedural, but they have a focus on procedures with understanding, connections, and multiple pathways to the solution. Students are required to actively engage with the material and analyze their thinking and understanding.

Higher-level tasks tend to lend themselves to tasks utilizing productive struggle, as the active engagement and deep connections being made are the basis of the challenge for the students. Without practice, it is very easy to begin to break down a high-level task into a series of lower-level tasks for students when they are stuck. This turns the productive struggle into simply seeking for the correct answer without connections. The teacher is given the task of selecting activities that ask students to think, discuss, and reason at a high level from the start.

Often, when students are first introduced to productive struggle in the mathematics classroom, their first reaction is to ask the teacher for the answer. "I'm stuck" or "I don't know where to start" are common phrases. The teacher's perspective is not the only one which must change for the effective use of productive struggle in the classroom. *Principles to Actions* (NCTM, 2014) outlines the new expectations for students in a classroom which emphasizes productive struggle.

First, and foremost, students must learn that worthwhile tasks will often take time and sometimes cause frustration, but perseverance is an important factor in success. In a world where instant gratification is becoming more and more common, this type of mind-set often must be taught explicitly to students. Students must also understand that correct solutions are not the only important part of a problem; the ability to explain reasoning and discuss the steps one took are also very important. As the age-old adage says, it's not the destination, but the journey, that matters.

Additionally, students are expected to ask questions of their peers or the teacher when they do not understand. Beyond this, students are expected to share their thinking with others even when they have no question. Productive struggle does not work in the classroom unless every student is making the learning their own. One of the hallmarks of active learning is the need for every student to be involved. This creates the need for a substantial shift in classroom expectations. Students also need to learn how to communicate their thinking and mathematical concepts, which is not as common in traditional mathematics classrooms. Students may need to be explicitly taught how to have these conversations before learning the mathematical material (NCTM, 2014).

Classrooms where productive struggle and discovery learning are implemented may well look chaotic to the outside observer. Smith and Stein (2011) provided the case study of an early-career teacher who, after collaborating with colleagues, implemented student-centered learning in her classroom. While observing the lesson, the principal noted that the class was "incoherent, with everyone doing his or her own thing" (2011, p. 90) before seeing the amount of work and thought the group of teachers put into the lesson. The aspects of discovery and struggle in the classroom lend themselves well to students working in small groups, and often do not align with traditional lecture-style activities.

This major change in both thinking and classroom activities will take substantial effort for teachers. Beyond the major shift in expectations and thinking in the classroom, teachers will need to redesign many aspects of their curriculum. The curriculum used for years will suddenly not fit with the expectations of the classroom. Generic worksheets that ask students to solve twenty or thirty problems repetitively or lecture-based lessons will need to be adapted to challenge students and allow for discussion. Higher-level tasks must be selected and aligned with the goals of the lesson.

Even when the preparation work is complete, curriculum and lesson plans are changed, and expectations are set within the classroom, there will be a significant amount of trial and error involved in the transition to productive struggle in the classroom. Student expectations in the classroom must be cultivated; what works for one class may not work for another. An activity that was supposed to be a significant challenge for students may end up being a trivial exercise that takes significantly less time than was scheduled.

On the flip side, an activity that might have been scheduled as an incidental review may pose a significant challenge to students and cause undue frustration. Upon using the new materials in front of a class, teacher expectations may need to be adjusted. This transition will not be easy, quick, or entirely without roadblocks. Teachers require extra time, resources, and collaboration time to change.

Ideally every teacher would experience the assistance of an expert in creating a classroom where active learning and productive struggle are integral. The input of college professors or lead teachers along with the collaboration of peers would help them create this type of environment, and then become experts themselves. However, this is not always, or even often, feasible. A professional-development program in which teachers listen to a speaker discuss these things for hours but do not act on it, is not a good option for making the transition.

The good news is that there are plenty of resources to help teachers and educators make the shift. While solitary reading of these materials without the opportunity to act on them may not be helpful, allowing groups of teachers to work through these materials together over a long period of time is critical. Collaboration is the key to understanding and growth.

PRINCIPLES AND STANDARDS FOR SCHOOL MATHEMATICS

NCTM has produced several iterations of a standards document for mathematics teaching. The first iteration, *Curriculum and Evaluation Standards* in 1989, was followed by *Professional Standards for Teaching Mathematics* in 1991, and *Assessment Standards for School Mathematics* in 1995.

Principles and Standards for School Mathematics, written in 2000, is a revised and updated version of NCTM's original standards. While not a curriculum, the standards are intended to lead policymakers and those who build curricula. Most state and national mathematics standards are influenced by the NCTM *Principles and Standards*.

The majority of the document is a list of standards, organized by grade band and topic. While these standards are helpful to teachers, especially as they create learning goals for the classroom, the most pertinent part for the purposes of teacher growth and collaboration is chapter 2. Chapter 2, the principles part of the document, "describes particular features of high-quality mathematics education" (NCTM, 2000). The six principles suggested by the NCTM are equity of experiences for all students, a coherent, understandable curriculum, effective teaching, active learning, assessment that supports learning goals, and use of technology. Each of the principles is explained in the chapter, along with suggestions as to how each can be applied.

In the teaching and learning principles, the emphasis is on supporting and creating a challenging but supportive classroom environment. Task selection, an important part of student-centered learning, is covered in the teaching principle. The learning principle suggests that "procedural fluency and conceptual understanding can be developed through problem solving, reasoning and argumentation" (NCTM, 2000, p. 21). These principles, along with the others, can be a springboard for teachers transitioning to student-centered learning.

Principles to Actions

Principles to Actions: Ensuring Mathematical Success for All (NCTM, 2014) is the first of a series of documents from NCTM that elaborate on the principles section of *Principles and Standards*. *Principles to Actions* takes the original NCTM standards and principles focusing on how they can be applied to the classroom. "Standards alone . . . will not realize the goal of high levels of mathematical understanding by all students. . . . *Principles to Actions* describes the conditions, structures and policies that must exist for all students to learn" (NCTM, 2014, p. vii).

The guiding principles set forth in *Principles to Actions* have been slightly updated from the year 2000 principles. All of the general principles are qualities found in an excellent mathematics program. First, the program puts an emphasis on both effective teaching strategies and meaningful learning through experiences that promote sense making and reasoning, as a general principle.

The second general principle is an emphasis on access to high-quality curriculum, support, effective teaching, and meaningful learning for all students. Third, the curriculum of such a program must lead students to connections between mathematical areas and the real world. Fourth, the program uses tools and technology effectively. Fifth, assessment is integral to teaching, includes a variety of sources, and is used for improvement of the program. Finally, the educators in the program hold themselves accountable for student learning and personal growth in teaching.

Each of the preceding guiding principles is explored in depth in an individual chapter in the book. Each chapter includes a chart of common productive and unproductive beliefs which underlie the topic. General principle 1, teaching and learning, is further broken down into eight teaching practices. NCTM terms the teaching which encapsulates these eight practices as ambitious teaching. These eight teaching practices are tied closely with the eight Standards for Mathematical Practice from the Common Core State Standards, including facilitating meaningful discourse, supporting productive struggle, and posing purposeful questions.

For each of these practices, illustrations are given, and there is a list of what teachers and students must do in the classroom to make the practice effective. General principles 2–6 compose the "Essential Elements" of an excellent mathematics program. For the Essential Elements, each chapter is laid out to include obstacles to implementation, ways to overcome the obstacles, an illustration, and a way to move the section into action in the classroom. Finally, *Principles to Actions* gives concrete ways that policymakers, teachers, and principals must act in order to bring each individual principle to fruition.

Taking Action

Taking Action: Implementing Effective Mathematical Teaching Practices takes the teaching practices that are outlined in *Principles to Actions* and expands upon them. The practices "describe intentional and purposeful actions that teachers take to support the engagement and learning of every student" (Smith, Steele, and Raith, 2017, p. 4). Available in grade bands K–5, 6–8, and 9–12, *Taking Action* describes actionable ways to implement the teaching practices appropriate for the grade level. The book is intended for teachers who wish to improve their teaching; the author also suggests the book for use by groups of teachers working together.

Each teaching principle is described in its own chapter. The chapters contain "Analyzing Teaching and Learning" sections that ask teachers to work through an activity that will set the stage for the chapter. The rationale for the various practices is described and the case study presented at the beginning of the book, or a new case study, is related to the principle that is the focus of the chapter. The chapters then summarize research on the principle and relate the principle to equity in the classroom. Finally the authors summarize the key points of the chapter and invite the reader to apply these points in the classroom through a "Taking Action in Your Classroom" activity to complete the chapter.

The book concludes by "Putting It All Together." The final chapters describe how the principles can interact and affect each other. The authors specifically discuss how lesson planning, reflection, and using equitable teaching in the classroom can pull all the teaching practices together and lead to mathematics classrooms where student-centered learning is emphasized. The teaching practices, including promoting mathematical discourse, promoting productive struggle, and posing purposeful questions, are particularly helpful to teachers intending to incorporate more student-centered learning into their classroom.

5 Practices for Orchestrating Productive Mathematics Discussions

Smith and Stein's (2011) *5 Practices for Orchestrating Productive Mathematics Discussions* focuses on the planning aspects that can introduce healthy discussion into the mathematics classroom. The five practices proposed are anticipating student responses, monitoring student responses, selecting students to present their work, sequencing displayed responses, and connecting the responses to the key idea of the lesson. Through a series of chapters and case studies illustrating the practices, Smith and Stein help teachers to build an environment that encourages productive discussion in the classroom.

Since the main focus is planning, this book is ideal for groups of teachers to work through when planning new class activities. While transitioning to a friendly productive-struggle classroom, teachers should introduce new activities into the classroom. Many of these activities may be group-based; all will include students working on their own. *5 Practices for Orchestrating Productive Mathematics Discussions* attempts to take the burden of improvising off teachers in the lesson and help them move it to the planning stages.

One of the greatest struggles in making productive discussion a norm in the classroom is encouraging the students to discuss among themselves, not just with the teacher, and shaping the discussion so that it is beneficial to student learning. Through the five practices, Smith and Stein (2011) encourage teachers to plan expected student responses and organize them into a logical order for presentation to the class. Additionally, each chapter has several *Active Engagement* sections for group discussion and interaction with the text.

TRU Framework

The Teaching for Robust Understanding (TRU) Framework is a framework for learning proposed by Alan Schoenfeld. The TRU Framework is meant to be a comprehensive set of five focus dimensions that can be used to create a classroom where "the students who emerge from that environment will be knowledgeable, flexible, and resourceful thinkers and learners" (Schoenfeld, 2006, p. 2). The focus dimensions are meant to be broad enough for significant professional-development opportunities, while not telling teachers how to teach, but rather providing a framework within which to work. Schoenfeld claimed, "professional learning communities that focus on what counts will produce sustained improvement in teaching and in student understanding" (2014, p. 3). The TRU framework provides the focus dimensions to allow this to happen.

The five focus dimensions for a strong learning environment from the TRU framework are the content available, the cognitive demand of the classroom tasks, the equitable nature of access to the content, students' ownership and identity in the classroom, and the use and inclusion of formative assessment in the classroom. The cognitive demand of the tasks must be high for productive struggle in the classroom; student identity in the classroom will influence the personal comfort level with engaging in productive discussion with classmates. TRU discusses what is meant by each of these dimensions and upon what should be the focus.

Unlike the other resources mentioned in this chapter, the TRU framework is found online and, as such, comes with additional resources and opportunities that are not always available in books. Each focus dimension is accompanied by a Conversation Guide, perfect for groups of educators to use to discuss and formulate ideas around each dimension. The conversations can be far-reaching: they can be used in both planning lessons and reflecting on lessons. There also are some content-specific conversation guides that focus on specific subjects, such as algebra; other content-specific conversation guides are being developed. Additionally, Observation Guides, meant specifically for planning and debriefing classroom observations, are available. These are helpful for guiding discussions among teachers who are implementing new strategies and having others observe them. Finally, the TRU framework is associated with the Mathematics Assessment Project, which adds additional resources like professional-development modules, both formative and summative assessment exemplars, and lessons.

SUMMARY

Implementing student-centered learning in the classroom is a time-consuming and challenging task. Allowing teachers to collaborate will help facilitate this process, making it less stressful and decreasing the risk felt by individual teachers as they step from their comfort zones. Fortunately, there are many resources available to support teachers in this transition. The resources previously listed are just a starting point; new resources are becoming available as the focus on student-centered learning increases.

Chapter Seven

Applying a Theoretical Basis to Drive Change

James Freemyer

PRE-READING REFLECTION

1. Why does leading significant change within an organization often fail?
2. What is the track record for change in the field of mathematics education?
3. What benefits are there to using a theoretical basis for leading change in a middle or high school setting?
4. How does one theoretical basis for change leadership apply in the school setting?
5. What steps should principals take once they agree to help teachers adapt their long-honored teaching approach?

WHAT TO EXPECT IN THIS CHAPTER

A blueprint for how successful change could occur in mathematics classrooms in the United States follows. The chapter advocates for change to occur at the local level, where the critical decisions are made. Local academic leaders are challenged to become involved in assisting mathematics teachers to adapt their pedagogical approach to better engage all students. The challenges of leading change at critical junctures are explored.

Black and Gregersen (2008) provide a theoretical basis for leading change. They begin by explaining that when "the old right thing becomes the new wrong thing" (p. 70), it is difficult for people to buy into the change initiative. They describe three barriers which are often present during a change initiative: (a) failure to see the need, (b) failure to move, and (c) failure to finish (Black and Gregersen, 2002, p. 43). People targeted for change often must grapple with four entities: (a) do the right thing and do it well; (b) discover that the right thing is now the wrong thing; (c) do the right thing but do it poorly at first; and (d) eventually do the new right thing well (Black and Gregersen, 2008, p. 14). To be successful, change must occur at the local level.

ALWAYS CHANGING, NEVER ARRIVING

Change in mathematics education has a storied path replete with failed attempts, from the new math era of the 1950–1960s, which saw a back-to-basics backlash, to the more recent Common Core approaches that politicians attack with dogmatic fervor. Such a seismic shift in the approach to teaching mathematics has not be easy in any country, anywhere in the world. This was evident in my research experiences in Indiana, Ireland, Great Britain, South Korea, and Japan.

The resistance to change in the United States is compounded by periodic failed attempts at drastic change throughout the decades. Teachers have become numb to the constant call to change; they simply want to continue to teach the way they were taught and the way they learned as they moved through the ranks. Failed attempts at change make this current initiative even more challenging. How can the United States compete in an international world by reaching out only to the best and brightest students who are capable of easily grasping complex ideas? The clear answer is simple: this country will fall behind developing countries that adapt to the changes more quickly and inspire their mathematics teachers to embrace the hard work of change.

THE ART OF LEADING CHANGE

If a government-backed, national mandate, such as the one in Ireland, had challenges and difficulties in initiating change, how can we as a nation hope to encourage major change approaches in our public schools? How can we create a systematic approach to changing and improving that addresses Stigler and Hiebert's (2009) concern for providing a "mechanism for getting better" (p. xix)? The answer, according to Black (2008) in his book *It Starts with One*, is that significant change must occur at the local level, not the national level.

Local leaders, including principals and mathematics department chairs, must drive the change at their level. Black (2008) insisted that change at the corporate level or national level simply does not address the many issues with which the rank and file grapple on a regular basis. Even when change is focused at the local level, the odds continue to be against significant changes occurring. Black and Gregersen (2008) estimated that 80 percent of change initiatives fail, even when carried out at the local level. Yet administering a significant change initiative at the local level is exactly what this nation needs as we seek to catch up with other nations that have embraced the new paradigm.

THE CULTURE OF CHANGE

It is left to local academic leaders, such as principals and department chairs, to learn the art of leading change and apply it in a real way to mathematics departments and teachers, helping them to embrace the challenges required of teaching mathematics in a more problem-based, conceptual way. However, changing the current culture is hard. Current paradigms are hard to overcome as teachers have spent ten, fifteen, twenty, or more years learning and perfecting their current teaching approach. Even if they embraced the change, like a teacher in Ireland did, implementing the change is hard and laborious.

According to Edgar Schein (2004), "the most intriguing aspect of culture as a concept is that it points to phenomena that are below the surface, that are unconscious. In that sense culture is to a group what personality or character is to an individual" (p. 8). Schein (2004) defined culture as "a pattern of shared basic assumptions that was learned by a group as it solved its problems of external adaptation and internal integration, that has worked well enough to be considered valid and, therefore, to be taught to new members as the correct way to perceive, think, and feel in relation to those problems" (p. 17).

According to Schein, for a leader to lead a change initiative they must observe the cultural artifacts that are seen on the surface and then seek to understand the espoused beliefs and values that reside under the surface. Yet that is still insufficient for effectively leading change. Leaders must probe even deeper into the culture and seek to understand underlying assumptions that drive the present culture.

Assuming that most principals were not mathematics teachers themselves, principals must spend considerable time learning the teachers' culture and guiding the change process if they hope to lead a successful change effort. Principals who effectively provide this structure for change will be addressing what Stigler and Hiebert (2009) recommended to create a mechanism for improvement. Ongoing teacher collaboration provides just such a mechanism.

Brain Barrier One: Failure to See

Black and Gregersen (2008) contended that change begins with understanding how individuals did the right thing very well. Due to changes in the environment, technology, global, or other issues, eventually the right thing becomes the wrong thing to do. Black and Gregersen (2008) provided an example.

Motorola was the industry leader in analog mobile phones in the 1980s. Everyone loved their phones, and Motorola was very good at producing their phones. But the environment shifted; Motorola was blinded by its current light (success) and opted not to change. Nokia developed digital cell phones while Motorola opted to put more money into developing even better analog phones. Change leaders must understand that people are reluctant to change when they have been successful at doing things one particular way (2014). "The old right thing becomes the new wrong thing" (Black and Gregersen 2014, p. 81). Failure to see the need for change is the first barrier to effective change.

Mathematics teachers are slow to see the need to teach more conceptually. The natural tendency is put more effort into teaching the old way even better. Mathematics teachers in Ireland believed that agreeing to change their approach was paramount to admitting they had been teaching wrong their entire careers.

While that is not at all what is transpiring now, principals must understand that motivating mathematics teachers to change is like early aviators trying to break through the sound barrier. Teachers' first reactions to low

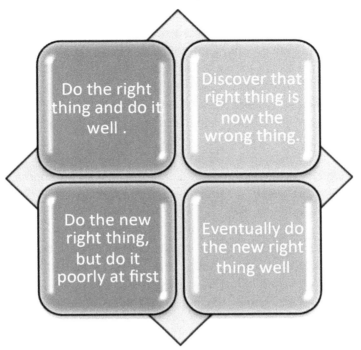

Figure 7.1. Difficulties of leading change. *Source:* Black and Gregersen (2014) by permission.

test scores are to give more quizzes, assess more often, or improve chapter tests to better align to standardized tests. Working harder becomes a substitute for working smarter.

Black and Gregersen (2014) contend that people are not blank slates. People hold mental maps of the right thing to do. Leaders must overcome the first barrier to change (brain barrier number one): individuals fail to see impending threats and opportunities. Individual workers hold on to those mental maps as the correct way to continue because "they are blinded by the light of what they already see—the mental maps that have worked for them in the past" (Black and Gregersen 2014, p. 5).

Part of the difficulty in successfully conducting a change process in an organization is due to the perspective of workers who tend to distort their own importance. Black and Gregersen (2014) noted that Barnes & Noble had a mental map that the best way to sell books was to build more brick-and-mortar buildings. Amazon viewed the market differently and began to sell books online without buildings. Barnes & Noble was blinded by their own light that said more buildings would produce more profitable book sales. They failed to see that the terrain had changed.

Leaders must create a sense of urgency if they are to succeed in changing workers' mental maps. Reviewing test results is only the first step in helping mathematics teachers who understand the need for change. In creating a sense of urgency about change, leaders begin by combining contrast and confrontation.

The academic leader should seek the best way to provide a high and compelling contrast between the old approach and a new approach. Helping mathematics teachers comprehend that teaching more conceptually engages more students in deep ways causes them to analyze and reflect on mathematics principles more often. Just how is the new approach different than the current approach? These differences must be emphasized.

The old paradigm to which most mathematics teachers hold often involves a "watch me, help me, now you try this" approach, where teachers have students mimic how they solve a problem. Teachers demonstrate how to factor a trinomial and then guide students to do the same thing. The problem is that students do not understand why they are factoring a trinomial and therefore they fail to comprehend the basic concepts.

Effective teachers now introduce a real-life problem and then use the mathematical processes to solve the problem. Students spend more time discovering solutions. Asking students to grapple with concepts rather than memorize procedures is a totally different paradigm. This paradigm requires more productive struggle by students as they seek to develop different approaches to solve the problem. This process takes significantly more in-class time.

Helping teachers understand how to engage students in conceptual understanding is much more taxing for teachers and administrators but vital to student growth. Make no mistake, nothing short of a major shift in culture will suffice. While students see mathematics as difficult, boring, disjointed facts, today's teachers must help students transcend that old, outdated image.

Research in Europe and Asia demonstrate that no student should have to spend one minute with a teacher who is not in love with their subject and passionate about sharing their excitement with a room full of students. Yet the obstacles are enormous. How many times have mathematics teachers heard how a student or a student's parents always hated mathematics?

But that mentality can be overcome in one, well-taught fifty-minute period. Academic leaders must insist that a positive, academic setting replete with challenges and growth permeates every single mathematics class. A classroom where students are safe to make mistakes and even see mistakes as stepping-stones to deeper understanding should be the hallmark of every school's mathematics department.

Creating Contrast

According to Black (2014), a leader should not assume that communicating one time about the changes will suffice. Repeated communication is in order. Portraying the contrast between what has worked in the past and what might work in the future is all important. Creating high contrast, according to Black and Gregersen (2008), involves (a) focusing on the core 20 percent of what is very different rather than what is slightly different, (b) enhancing (even slightly exaggerating) the simple description between the old and the new, and (c) creating visual images of the old and the new so that the contrast is understood as more than mere words.

Black and Gregersen (2014) recommended creating high-impact confrontation by repeating the message of the new and focusing on the core contrasts. Black and Gregersen (2014) suggested that one "take time and energy to identify the core 20 percent that accounts for 80 percent of the problems rather than the easier approach of working with all the factors of change" (p. 68).

Confrontation

Academic leaders at the local level must provide assistance and training for teachers to learn and grow. In Ireland that training entailed every single mathematics teacher in the country attending ten workshops during the course of two years to ensure that every teacher in the country understood the expected changes. Principals must ensure that teachers understand the new approach and have time to plan and carry out the changes. That would require principals to find ways to provide release time for mathematics teachers to plan and execute the new approaches.

When teachers see the commitment to this extra planning time that academic leaders provide, they will realize the importance of the proscribed changes. There is no substitute for principals observing the attempts at growth with these new approaches by observing practices in live classrooms and providing the always-needed encouraging word. Local encouragement is a main reason that effective change is best implemented at the classroom level.

Brain Barrier Two: Failure to Move

Brain barrier number two is the failure to move. Black and Gregersen explored why the majority of change projects fail even if a sense of urgency is established and a clear contrast is made. Seeing that the old right thing is now wrong is only half of the battle. Followers must also see the new right thing. If the new right thing is not clear, followers will fail to move.

Take the example of Xerox. They made large copiers for businesses, but Canon began making small copiers for individuals. At first Xerox failed to admit that the old right thing had become the new wrong thing. "Customers needed document solutions, not just copiers. Customers needed to be grouped by industry need . . . rather than geography (territories) as in the past" (Black and Gregersen, 2014, p. 176).

The mental map for many Xerox employees was too difficult to grasp. When it became more than obvious that they needed to shift from the territorial approach, they continued to struggle because they could not see a clear path based on the new paradigm. Black and Gregersen (2014) noted that employees must not only see the new approach, but they must believe in a new approach that will take them from doing the right thing poorly to doing it well. Helping followers believe involves:

- making sure that others see the destination clearly;
- giving followers the skills, resources, and tools to reach the destination; and
- delivering valuable rewards along the journey (Black and Gregersen, 2014).

Being Willing to Do the Job Poorly at First

The importance of giving mathematics teachers the necessary skills, resources, and tools to change cannot be overstated. What works in a school system across town may not work elsewhere. Teachers required time to collaborate, experiment, and reflect on new approaches. Again this requires a commitment of time and resources to allow teachers to collaborate with each other.

Teachers must come to grips with an important fact: teaching that involves more student-talking than teacher-talking will require time for growth and experimentation. When teachers first learn their profession, it is not uncommon to spend excessive hours in transitioning from being a college student to being a teacher in the classroom. Most teachers simply cannot invest that kind of time again as they shift to a new approach.

Teachers should not be expected to do this retraining on their own time like a first-year teacher. Adapting to this new paradigm that involves students in productive struggle and more of a discovery approach takes time to master. Teachers will do it poorly at first. This can be discouraging. Unless someone is there praising their persistence and good effort, teachers will quickly revert back to familiar, seeming successful approaches that they have perfected through the years. Research in Ireland affirmed this conclusion.

The ideal approach to such a dramatic change is frequent collaboration with colleagues. If administrators provide the time and guidance for such collaboration, then teachers can be expected to begin a slow process of sustainable change. Leaders must provide the time for collaboration before rank and file teachers can be expected to buy in. Expecting major change from teachers without an investment in time and training is simply irrational.

Many teachers began teaching in a culture where the teacher's classroom was their personal domain, not to be impinged upon except for the annual principal observation. Teachers have become accustomed to more frequent observations, but wholesale traffic of colleagues observing and dialoging would require a slow, well-developed implementation. Schools in Asia, which have committed to such collaboration, have reaped the rewards.

Clarke and Hollingsworth's (2002) framework addressed this issue. It provides for collaboration as teachers shape their learning through external stimuli followed by local experimentation and salient outcomes to change cultural beliefs and attitudes. Their model follows.

Goldsmith, Doerr, and Lewis (2014, p. 5) reviewed 106 articles related to professional learning of mathematics teachers that reinforce the

The Change Environment

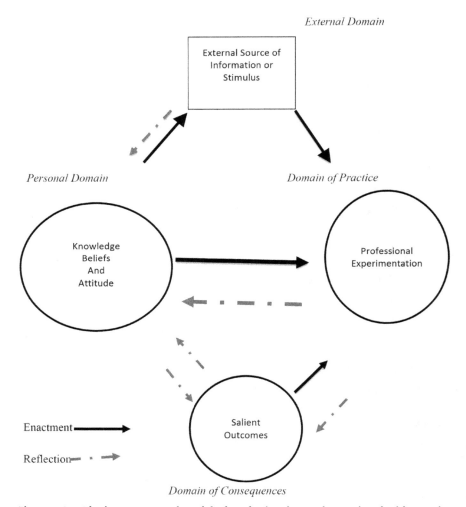

Figure 7.2.   The interconnected model of professional growth. Reprinted with permission from Hilary Hollingsworth; Clarke and Hollingsworth (2002).

need for teacher experimentation, collaboration, and reflection. They cited Clarke and Hollingsworth's model for guiding teacher learning approaches. This research-based approach to teacher growth provides an effective framework for teachers who are forced to adapt their long-held beliefs about effective teaching to a framework based upon a top-down, nationwide decision that requires significant change to their teaching approach. This research-based approach can help promote a Professional Learning Community.

Such a collaborative community could provide a platform for enriched dialogue regarding curriculum, assessment, and instructional approaches. If individual teacher growth can improve students' chances of advancement, how much more could entire mathematics departments' collaboration provide fertile ground for teacher progress? The impact on the curriculum, assessment, and instruction being aligned with current research could be formidable.

Brain Barrier Number Three: Failure to Finish

According to Black and Gregersen (2014), failure to finish, brain barrier three, happens because employees become tired, and lost, and, therefore, do not go fast enough or far enough. Achieving success requires champions in place to reinforce and encourage the first few times that seeds of change are planted and to applaud the first few steps in a walk of faith. Success requires monitoring progress and communicating individual and collective improvement (Black and Gregersen, 2014).

Data are necessary to drive the change process, allowing leaders to know when to champion success and when to adjust the process. Product data must be analyzed on a regular basis. Opinion surveys, focus groups, individual interviews, and student learning statistics all provide data that allow the leadership to monitor and adjust the change process. Any change initiative should have a limited amount of key elements to monitor. Black and Gregersen (2014) described considerations for creating and monitoring the change process:

- identify key elements to measure,
- determine a method of measurement,
- determine the appropriate interval of measurement,
- develop baseline data, and
- determine target results.

Finally, stakeholders require encouragement and assistance from the leaders most closely associated with their position during the time they are attempting the new right thing. When participants begin the new right thing, they will do it poorly at first. So they work hard, try the new thing, and pretty much have nothing to show for it at first. Change requires time, work, and optimistic perseverance.

Having the superintendent or the school board behind the change project is nice, but participants require encouragement from their direct supervisors or close colleagues. When one pays for a weight-loss process and starts to eat differently, at first the results can be very slow. One might make it through the first week and, yes, lose a few pounds; but one does not look much different at the beginning. Yet that is the time one most needs extra encouragement to work through the struggles.

Academic leaders must provide the unequivocally necessary time for teachers to grapple with these new approaches. Time is necessary for planning lessons, developing the lessons, and then reflecting on what worked and what did not. Reflection must focus on student learning and possible adaptations that could and should occur during the lesson, not just the following day. Schools in Europe and Asia that understood this were the most successful in the new approach.

Providing opportunities for teachers to collaborate with peers in the process can reinvigorate their own excitement and enthusiasm for teaching that can diminish through the years. Teachers in Ireland repeatedly voiced the need for extra time to plan new teaching approaches and more time in the classroom to allow students to experience productive struggle. This was mentioned by almost 70 percent of teachers who responded to the nationwide survey. Flexible scheduling of course periods was critical to effective growth (Freemyer, Fitzmaurice, Johnson, 2016).

SUMMARY

Leading a major change initiative can be the most challenging leadership experience one has ever encountered. Often teachers will nod their head in agreement when leaders discuss the need for change. Teachers can provide supportive comments as leaders detail the plan for change.

However, inside they can be consciously or unconsciously willing to undercut the process when the going gets rough. Taking a systematic approach to change, such as what has been discussed in this chapter, greatly increases the odds that new techniques will be given a real opportunity to succeed. As teachers work through the changes leaders might ask, will all this effort really pay off?

Chapter Eight

Exemplars of Professional Development

Dave Klanderman

PRE-READING REFLECTION

1. Among the mathematics teachers at your school, how would you categorize their ability and willingness to transition to a focus on more conceptual teaching and learning?
2. What barriers might exist that might prevent some of your teachers from making this transition and how might you enable them to overcome these barriers?
3. What local, state, and national resources might help you to leverage change within your school building?
4. Are there any local schools that may provide models for a more conceptually oriented mathematics instructional paradigm?

WHAT TO EXPECT IN THIS CHAPTER

Principals and other decision makers who have made it this far in the book have demonstrated a willingness to move forward with the necessary transformation that will shift the teaching and learning of mathematics to a more conceptual approach. The current chapter seeks to equip these leaders with tools to help identify the different types of teachers at their schools. It provides a series of vignettes to describe hypothetical teachers who exemplify each of five different types of teachers. In each case, this teacher's willingness and ability to change are described and suggestions are given for the optimal strategies to motivate and support teachers in this particular category.

Having analyzed the strengths, challenges, and potential of their current mathematics teaching staff, principals must next explore models for accomplishing the necessary transformation. This chapter highlights multiple initiatives at local, district, state, and national levels. While meant to be examples for these different levels, these initiatives may provide school leaders with key resources or possibly ideas to pursue with similar initiatives that are more readily available in the specific context for that leader's local school community. The major conclusion is that principals must provide ongoing support and release time for teachers to make and sustain this transformation in their classroom teaching.

Overall, this chapter seeks to provide school leaders with the diagnostic tools to identify the unique strengths and challenges possessed by different types of teachers at their schools. It also provides an overview of a series of initiatives that have the potential to support the process of transformation and to better equip school leaders to succeed in this major undertaking.

BACKGROUND AND CONTEXT

Recent measures of mathematical achievement by students in the United States document limited mastery of problem solving and more conceptual, as compared to procedural, understanding of mathematics, as reported by the National Assessment of Educational Progress (NAEP, 2018). Comparisons to developed countries around the world have shown the United States to be average or worse (cf. TIMSS, 2015). In response to these data, the mathematics education community has called for a greater focus on conceptual learning, as seen in *Principles and Standards for School Mathematics* (2000) and *Principles to Actions: Ensuring Mathematical Success for All* (2014).

This chapter argues that a collaborative transformation of mathematics teachers is required to enable them to prepare K–12 students for a competitive workplace in the current and coming decades. Specifically, principals, superintendents, school board, and other stakeholders must provide the necessary financial support and scaffolded encouragement to facilitate this transformation among the teaching staff in their schools.

School administrators are being asked to work with mathematics teachers as they take on this tremendous challenge to not just adapt their teaching approach but to totally redefine it. Yet the challenge for principals is just as daunting. Most schools have a mix of very skilled mathematics teachers who naturally engage all students in meaningful learning experiences and those who fall way short of effective teaching.

The research indicates that some teachers are effective when providing high expectations and problem-based approaches but fall short in areas of regularly engaging all students, building effective student/teacher relationships, motivating students to attempt challenging problems, and inspiring students by going the extra mile in their quest to succeed. Others are great at relationships but not as effective with high expectations. Principals are tasked with helping all mathematics teachers check all the teacher effectiveness boxes.

This chapter helps frame these key questions principals and department chairs grapple with on a regular basis. The majority of schools have work to do within the mathematics departments if the goal of inspiring more students to seek careers in science, technology, engineering, and mathematics (STEM) is to be attained. Let us look at some fictional mathematics teachers and contemplate how to inspire real faculty development and growth.

KNOWING YOUR AUDIENCE: CASE STUDIES OF FIVE TYPES OF MATHEMATICS TEACHERS

Since not all teachers are the same, it would be reasonable to conclude that a one-size-fits-all approach to staff development might be ineffective in achieving the goal of conceptual learning in mathematics classrooms. Principals and other leaders of change must differentiate their approaches to build on the unique talents, backgrounds, and learning styles of their mathematics faculty. However, as research in mathematics learning progressions have taught us (e.g., Barrett, Sarama, and Clements, 2017), learners tend to cluster in several groups rather than to demonstrate truly unique qualities in every case.

For this reason, case studies are provided that will highlight a total of five types of mathematics teachers and their readiness for change. In each case, a hypothetical example will offer insights in ways to provide scaffolding for a specific type of teacher to achieve a transformation to teaching and learning that is more conceptual, more inquiry-based, and more focused on relational understanding (Skemp, 1978).

Tasha

Tasha is known for being on the cutting edge of most innovations in technology, in teaching, and in life as a whole. While many colleagues were still dependent on proprietary software, like Geometer's Sketchpad, she immediately jumped on the bandwagon for open-source alternatives like GeoGebra. In fact, Tasha perseveres through beta-testing new technologies and is comfortable working through bugs, glitches, and other shortcomings of the initial rollouts of the latest trends in teaching.

As a first adopter, she should be one of your very first recruits as a leader of change in a school. She should be provided with the support to attend workshops and conferences that assume participants are ready and able to implement rapid change in the teaching and learning environment. She naturally has the uncommon mix that marries high expectations, an understanding of problem-based learning, and a strong passion to connect with students.

One must capitalize on her enthusiasm by equipping her to lead as a mentor for her colleagues. Once she has mastered the transition, she will be a walking advertisement for the kind of change that is sought. Consider naming her a lead teacher with corresponding reduction in daily teaching duties to allow her to observe and coach other colleagues at her school. Teachers of this first type do not need to be convinced to pursue the change, but they will be more impactful with the rest of a school if they are fully supported before, during, and after receiving high-quality training in programs similar to those that will be described in detail at the end of the chapter.

Dan

Dan supports the overall goal of shifting to a teaching and learning environment that places a greater focus on conceptual understanding. As such, he is an eager participant in any professional-development activities that may be offered. At the same time, he has less experience in the types of dynamic changes that are second nature for teachers like Tasha. For this reason, leaders must provide encouragement and affirmation of his incremental progress along the way.

There are certain to be setbacks in the early as well as later stages of the transition to more conceptual, inquiry-based teaching. If no ongoing encouragement is provided, he may lose his enthusiasm for making the required changes and may revert to his prior approaches to teaching, which have, at least in his own view, proven successful in helping his students learn, albeit more procedurally and instrumentally than relationally and conceptually.

It is probably less about the financial support and other monetary incentives for moving ahead with the transition and much more about a simple word of appreciation for the effort, an acknowledgment of incremental progress, and an occasional word of encouragement to persevere in the face of setbacks, especially at the beginning of the process. Leaders may consider enlisting Tasha to help with this support network, but must remember that the leader of change sets the tone for the teaching staff to follow.

Andrea

Andrea considers herself open to potential changes and innovations in teaching and learning. However she is a bit skeptical about the latest fad in education and is therefore cautious about moving forward with the necessary training and transition. For teachers similar to Andrea, the leaders' role must be to provide evidence of the success of conceptually based learning. Citing relevant examples from other countries that have demonstrated improved performance on comprehensive mathematics examples after adopting such a shift in the teaching and learning paradigm. One may wish to consult chapter 9 in this book for more specifics.

If there are any examples from school districts in one's home state, particularly those that would be familiar to Andrea, offering to connect her with teachers at these schools will let her see the success firsthand. One must first prove to Andrea the potential for improved learning that will result from making this transformation. Then, and perhaps only then, will she be a willing participant who truly desires to make the necessary changes, some of which may require her to alter her understanding of the role and best practices of the mathematics teacher.

Dawn

Dawn might best be described as a teacher stuck in familiar patterns in the classroom environment. Whether or not she has proven to be successful is less relevant than the fact that she is resistant to change, any change whatsoever. For Dawn, a leader should develop scaffolding that allows her to start small and experience some immediate successes. She will likely benefit from having Tasha come alongside and provide very specific assistance for making initial steps in the right direction.

Tasha could serve as an accountability mentor who would maintain ever-increasing expectations for Andrea's growth while simultaneously making a conscious effort to praise early successes and offer advice for taking the next step in the journey. Once again, evidence of how colleagues have been able to succeed would be relevant; but the encouragement should be differentiated to focus on the precise points where Andrea has exhibited some growth and the steps that are within her zone of proximal development (cf. Vygotsky, as cited in Smith and Stein, 2011) rather than expecting her to develop at the same pace as the types of teachers described earlier in this chapter.

Dawn, and colleagues like her, will eventually be the greatest success stories and will be able to present convincing arguments to parents and students. However this role for Dawn cannot happen until she has progressed along the transition, at a pace comfortable to her and with scaffolding at key moments.

John

John disagrees with the goal of the entire process. He is a firm believer that students must develop and maintain computational fluency at all costs. Problem solving and conceptual understanding are seen as unnecessary and, at best, subservient to rote memorization of key facts and ongoing demonstration of fluency with computational algorithms. New fads come and new fads go. Good teaching has remained a constant.

As a leader of change in a school, one must be realistic about the potential for John to make the transition. In fact, it is not only John's limited likelihood of success that should be of concern. More importantly, John may have a negative impact on the enthusiasm and morale of the other mathematics teachers in a building. This, in turn, may impede the growth of some of John's colleagues and, by extension, students having John or these colleagues as teachers.

Essentially, one may have to make the difficult choice of facilitating John's move to a profession other than teaching. This may require an involved review process, but the difficulties in making this change are less than those that would remain if John were allowed to negatively impact the entire initiative. Sometimes, one simply must move in a different direction.

TAPPING INTO YOUR RESOURCES

Having made the decision to lead this process of transformation among teachers at a local school, the principal, superintendent, or other decision makers must choose from among several available programs. The specific choice will be influenced by existing resources at the local school, available funds, and a careful analysis of the types of mathematics teachers present at the school as identified by the hypothetical case studies discussed earlier. This next section analyzes various possible programs, noting distinctives, possible advantages, and even limitations in each case. As an organizational framework, this analysis would proceed from the most local option to those that are more national in scope.

School-Based Resources

For some schools, existing support personnel are available to facilitate professional development among the mathematics teaching staff. Math coaches can offer support and encouragement at the individual level, and this may prove to be the most important feature of the transformation process. These coaches must be prepared to lead this transformation; this preparation may take the form of workshops at regional and national conferences, which will be explored in a later section.

Ideally these coaches will have demonstrated teaching effectiveness in ways that develop conceptual learning among mathematics students in grades K–12. It would be helpful for them to know the different types of mathematics teachers discussed earlier as well as ways to motivate teachers in each situation in the development process.

Support for Collaboration

A second common type of support person in some local schools is a math curriculum specialist. While this person normally helps individual teachers to maximize the potential of available textbooks, technology, and other classroom resources, the same person may have a background in pedagogical strategies designed to promote conceptual or relational understanding (Skemp, 1978). In fact, this specialist can work collaboratively with the math coaches to provide overall leadership in the transformation process.

This leadership may include meetings of all mathematics teachers in the school building that are held at key points along the way. For both math coaches and math curriculum specialists, it should not be assumed that these personnel have prior experience with teaching that promotes conceptual learning or that they necessarily support such a transformation. If this is not the case, then the principal must decide whether these support personnel are able to lead the process, with or without additional training that might be obtained through programs that will be outlined.

One key to utilizing mathematics coaches and mathematics curriculum specialists is providing additional time off for teacher joint-planning sessions and teacher joint-observation opportunities. Creating a joint lesson plan and then providing opportunities for team observations makes for rich discussion especially as teachers experiment with conceptual teaching approaches. Effective schools in Great Britain, South Korea, and Japan were adept at setting aside time for joint teaching experiences that improve the skills of all.

District-Level Resources

It has been said that imitation is the greatest form of flattery. In the case of high-quality mathematics instruction that achieves conceptual learning among students, following the lead of nearby schools that have already produced results is a logical choice. For example, principals at such schools may be willing and perhaps even eager to share the secrets of their success. This might include providing math coaches or math curriculum specialists to lead workshops at another school. Teachers from this successful school may be able to meet with colleagues from another school.

Even better, it may be possible to facilitate ways for teachers at the target school to observe the classrooms of the already successful school. This modeling in realistic classroom situations can be a powerful professional-development tool. It is worth noting that such initiatives will require funding, whether these funds are used to provide substitutes in the target school or to compensate the teachers and support personnel at the successful school.

Advanced Placement (AP) courses can provide a template for such collaborative experiences. As the time for the standardized test approaches, experts in AP frequently provide teaching tips and ideas at Saturday-morning sessions targeted at helping teachers focus on key components. Why could we not do similar sessions for improving teaching at the Algebra II level? Local school districts who are serious about improving mathematics test scores must provide resources to make meaningful collaboration a reality.

Another option at the district level may be a program designed to provide intensive professional development for classroom teachers over a prolonged time period. One such program recently was begun at the Kent Intermediate School District (ISD) in Grand Rapids, Michigan. The program is designed to offer professional development and ongoing support in best practices to mathematics teachers, including an emphasis on conceptual learning. The initial phase during the 2018–2019 school year includes approximately two dozen student teaching interns from several local colleges and universities.

These preservice teachers meet monthly to learn about best practices, share experiences from their clinical placements, and develop goals for the following weeks and months of classroom teaching. This program will next expand to in-service teachers in the following school year.

The eventual goal is to follow these preservice teachers into their future classrooms to document success in learning among their K–12 students. Those teachers who demonstrate success will also be invited to return to the Kent ISD program as teaching mentors. They will then have the opportunity to "pay it forward" by mentoring the next generation of student teaching interns as well as serving as role models for those in-service teachers who are beginning the process of transformation. This district-level initiative receives funding from the Michigan Department of Education. Similar programs may be available for school districts in other states.

State-Level Resources

Although the local school building and surrounding district might be the first place to look for resources, other options may be provided by other sources within the state. This next section discusses two sample programs in the state of Michigan. While these specific programs may not be offered in other states, it is likely that local colleges and universities may provide similar programs to help mathematics teachers develop their abilities to promote conceptual learning. Some resources are available online, so state boundaries are not always an issue.

Title II funds are provided at the state and national level to assist schools that are defined as *high-need* or those whose enrolled students come from families experiencing poverty or other low socioeconomic status (SES) conditions. The state of Michigan provided some of these funds during a twelve-year period to Dr. Janice Koop, a professor at Calvin College specializing in mathematics education at the elementary and middle school levels. She developed programs for in-service teachers in the Grand Rapids area, focusing on public schools as well as private and charter schools that met the Title II criteria established for the grant.

In each case she and a colleague provided focused professional development for all mathematics teachers at the school during a period of fifteen to eighteen months. Typically, the first step was a weeklong summer institute in which the in-service teachers collaborated on a variety of learning activities, many based upon appropriate manipulatives; some sourced from Sherry Parrish's *Number Talks* (2010). All required the teachers to reflect on both their own learning experiences as well as ways that similar activities with their own students might lead to both deeper conceptual learning and the eliciting of their students' thought processes.

Teachers were given a stipend for the summer institute using grant funds and were allowed to keep print resources discussed during the meetings. During the following school year, Dr. Koop and her colleague visited classrooms of participating teachers to offer encouragement and additional support. Five full-day in-service meetings were held throughout the year. Each of these meetings was supported by the building principal, who agreed to provide substitute teachers as necessary. Finally, a second five-day summer institute was held at the end of that school year.

There are two important outcomes of these programs in the period of more than a decade. First, significant growth in mathematical content knowledge was documented for the teachers of all but one of the numerous schools that participated. Thus deeper mathematics learning resulted from the focused work to equip teachers to employ teaching strategies designed to elicit more conceptual understanding. Second, and perhaps equally important, all the participating schools demonstrated significantly greater positive attitudes by teachers toward the discipline of mathematics and personal self-efficacy in teaching mathematical concepts. By these standards, this initiative shows success sustained with both public and private schools.

A second example of a statewide initiative is based at the University of Michigan. A program named Teaching Works has identified a total of nineteen high-leverage teaching practices. Some of these practices focus more on personal behaviors and relationships: building respectful relationships with students, talking about a student with parents or other caregivers, and the like. Others focus primarily on assessment, such as selecting and designing formal assessments of student learning and providing oral and written feedback to students.

However, other practices are aimed directly at the development of conceptual learning among students. In particular, teachers are called on to "elicit and interpret individual students' thinking" and to "diagnose particular common patterns of student thinking and development in a subject-matter domain." Many colleges and universities have agreed to these high-leverage practices. In each case, specific practices are identified as a focus area among their preservice teachers. In turn, this is leading to the modification of course assignments and field and clinical practices to help preservice teachers develop in these key high-leverage practices.

Like the Kent ISD program described earlier, the initial focus on preservice teachers should help infuse the teaching staffs at local schools with new teachers who are ready to implement these high-leverage practices. The next step for this program would be similar initiatives with local K–12 schools, and principals would be encouraged to consult related websites and online resources as they design and choose programs to facilitate transformation among their own mathematics teachers.

For both of these statewide initiatives, there is a crucial role for principals in the process. It is worth noting that Dr. Koop exercised control over the choice of schools that would participate in the Title II grant; she deliberately opted for schools in which the principal and teaching staff expressed strong support for the potential of the program. Principals with less-than-favorable views toward this initiative were quickly removed from the list of potential participating schools. Similarly, principals must take the initiative to seek out resources related to the Teaching Works program sponsored by the University of Michigan. Thus, principals must fully support the transformation process and to rally support among the teaching staff.

Nationwide Resources

There are several programs that have a more national scope. Most of these programs have local affiliates that would serve as the contact point for a local school. This final section explores three examples. The first offers resources of sessions, workshops, and short courses through professional conferences. The second describes a mathematics teaching circle. The third extends the second idea to K–12 students via a math circle. While all these specific examples are based in the United States, it would be worth searching for similar programs in other countries for readers in an international setting.

The National Council of Teachers of Mathematics (NCTM) hosts a multiday annual convention each April at rotating locations around the United States. Regional conferences offer similar experiences three or four times annually at a somewhat smaller venue. Each of these conferences are attended by hundreds or thousands of mathematics educators, including those who teach in grades K–12, support personnel for these same levels, and college and university faculty members.

Most conferences offer individual sessions, more in-depth workshops, and sometimes longer multi-session courses. Among the topics of current interest are those focused on professional development that targets conceptual learning among K–12 students. While single sessions or even in-depth multi-session courses are probably not sufficient to support the transformation of individual teachers, these conferences may still prove to be a valuable resource.

Principals may choose to send math coaches, curriculum specialists, and even lead teachers to attend multiple sessions on a topic. These experts can then share their knowledge at extended and multi-session professional-development workshops for all mathematics teachers at a school. It is also possible that valuable networking opportunities may offer resources for future professional development at a local school level. If a workshop is led by a dynamic speaker who describes more in-depth resources available at the local level, then this contact information can provide the principal with a potential resource for future in-service opportunities.

Another nationwide effort to help teachers focus on conceptual learning in their mathematics classrooms is led by the American Institute of Mathematics (AIM). This organization has provided seed grant funds to local leadership groups to form Mathematics Teacher Circles (MTCs). A MTC is a collaboration of college or university faculty members with multiple K–12 mathematics teachers to provide both extended summer institutes and monthly sessions for K–12 mathematics teachers.

Most sessions start with one or more challenge problems and then move to an extended, problem-solving activity facilitated by a lead teacher, often a member of the leadership group for the local MTC. These activities are designed for collaborative work among the teachers in which conceptual rather than procedural understanding is the primary focus.

At the completion of each of these sessions, teachers are encouraged to reflect on their own teaching practices and to explore whether this particular activity, or others more suited to their own grade level but in a similar problem-solving context, might be implementable in their respective classrooms. Most MTCs offer a full-day or multiday summer institute consisting of multiple sessions based upon this same format. These institutes serve as launch events for the monthly meetings scheduled during the school year, often on a weekday evening with a light dinner provided.

The funds necessary to maintain the operation of these MTCs are relatively modest and often funded by private donors, with typically little or no cost to the K–12 teachers or their associated schools. At least one study has documented growth in positive attitudes and willingness to experiment with these approaches to classroom learning among the participating teachers (Clark et al., 2018). There are more than one hundred MTCs in the United States, so there is very likely one relatively close to a local school. If not, then a principal should contact a nearby university to propose a partnership among a few teachers from both institutions to start one. An extensive collection of high-quality MTC activities is available at AIM's website.

A third type of program in this category of national scope is an extension of the previous one to K–12 students. Math Circles (MCs) host regular sessions that focus on similar problem-solving activities. However, the audiences for these sessions are K–12 students. Programs are most often run by a college or university, such as those hosted at Calvin College and the University of Michigan.

Sometimes a weeklong summer camp serves as a launch event for a weekly program scheduled during the school year. At one level, these MCs provide principals with a way to engage selected students with high-quality mathematical tasks requiring conceptual thinking and collaborative work. Initially students participating in the math club at the local school or perhaps students enrolled in an honors math course might be recruited to participate. However, the potential impact of a MC is more far-reaching.

Lead teachers or others who have made progress in the transformation to more conceptual learning in mathematics teaching may volunteer to assist at a MC session or may simply attend to observe the K–12 students engaged in solving the problems. The K–12 students develop skills in channeling their enthusiasm and energy toward team goals of solving problems that initially appear very difficult. This perseverance addresses one of the Standards of Mathematical Practice that accompany the Common Core State Standards for Mathematics. The programs described in this section are national in scope or design, but they also have local affiliates that could address the needs of teachers and students at the local school level.

SUMMARY

As can be seen from the previous discussion, there are a wide variety of options that decision makers might select for this transformation process. It is possible that a combination of programs, rather than a solitary one, may provide the greatest chance of success. Some of the programs require significant monetary commitments; all of them require professional-development time, perhaps supported by in-service activities, summer institutes, release time facilitated by substitute teachers, or possibly a combination of approaches. The leaders of this process must offer encouragement throughout by recognizing early successes, celebrating later student-learning gains, and treating the teaching staff as committed professionals.

The next chapter provides a blueprint for leaders describing key ideas for effective student engagement. Chapter 9 delineates how these approaches have been observed in a successful school in Scotland, South Korea, and one in Japan. The synergy and excitement of their mathematics teachers have yielded considerable success in standardized assessments. Their hallmark is that teachers collaborate regularly. The students enter a climate of high expectations, a positive and supportive environment where students fully expect to succeed. *The excitement and enthusiasm are contagious.* The level of teacher collaboration, where the focus on what helps students learn far exceeds the issue of classroom autonomy and teacher anonymity, will be described next.

Chapter Nine

Examples of Collaboration Observed in Europe and Asia

James Freemyer

PRE-READING REFLECTION

1. The idea of teachers working together to make significant changes in their teaching approach sounds good on paper, but where has it actually worked?
2. How does a principal systematically approach the idea of enhancing teacher collaboration?
3. What investments in money would be required to assist mathematics teachers execute a major shift in their teaching approach?
4. How are countries around the world handling the global need for mathematics teachers to adapt their overall approach to teaching more conceptually?

WHAT TO EXPECT IN THIS CHAPTER

Principals now realize the complexity involved in helping mathematics teachers consistently make a major shift in the teaching approach. Research conducted in Europe and Asia affirmed that academic leaders around the globe are focused in helping all mathematics teachers regularly teach from a conceptual approach. Major mandates from national leaders have failed to impact teacher practices at the local level. Real-life examples from interviews and observations at model schools demonstrate evident and significant improvement in student engagement when teaching are encouraged and assisted to collaborate with colleagues. In both

Europe and Asia, local leaders are committed to providing encouragement and dialogue opportunities to support classroom teacher collaboration resulting in a renewed teacher excitement.

Principals who dream of mathematics classrooms replete with engaged students interacting in collaborative ways as students grapple with key concepts now have a process available to help fulfill this fantasy. Providing mathematics teachers with the capacity to collaborate with peers in an effort to grapple with key concepts has increased teacher effectiveness in Europe and in Asia. Providing segments of teacher release time for joint lesson planning, observation, lesson analysis, and expanded use of technology have proven successful in transforming mathematics departments into a catalyst for renewed growth. If the goal is exciting more students to take more advanced courses in mathematics, model schools in Europe and Asia provide the blueprint.

A LOOK ABROAD

Observing some of the most effective schools in Indiana, Ireland, Great Britain, South Korea, and Japan provided a surprising and unique viewpoint on how some of our most effective teachers make a positive difference. The goal of this book was to discover what better teachers are doing and then find ways to infect other teachers with the same enthusiasm that can lead to more students continuing in the course sequence for advanced mathematics courses. That will not happen unless students experience the passion of the teacher. Specific schools in Scotland, Japan, and South Korea were exemplary in inspiring students to pursue upper-level mathematics courses. What are key characteristics of truly effective schools? A deeper look at these schools is in order.

MODEL SCHOOL IN SCOTLAND

It is not surprising that, at the time of this research, the school in Scotland was rated in the top five secondary schools in Scotland based on results on standardized tests. When they had an opening for a new mathematics teacher, more than one hundred qualified applicants sought the position.

The excitement around mathematics education at the school was palpable, even factoring in that a foreign researcher was visiting. Would you like to draw the curtain back and see how they have been so successful? Let us take a closer look.

Leadership Approach

The principal set the tone and provided unwavering support for efforts of members of the mathematics department. He was in the shadows as far as the school visit, but not in the light of day as far as his investment and commitment in substantive efforts of the mathematics (which they call maths) department.

His leadership supported numerous initiatives, including faculty chair release time: (a) to observe and coach each mathematics teacher five times per year; (b) to coordinate collaboration on the development of joint lessons plans, allowing teachers time to discuss lesson approaches and then to assess effectiveness; (c) to organize teacher joint observations of each other's classes once every other week, promoting collaboration; (d) to provide time for teacher-led mathematics on-site help sessions during lunch, after school, on Saturday; (e) live, online learning help sessions; (f) an action research approach to quantify academic effectiveness: and (g) ongoing faculty development. The investment in teachers paid big dividends.

Teacher-with-teacher collaboration was built into a regular schedule. The extra time for teacher-with-teacher collaboration, in the year of the visit, was aided by the government providing an additional teacher in compliance with the law that supports mathematics teachers by guaranteeing each new teacher who majors in mathematics education a job for their first year whether or not a school has a need. That extra teacher allowed for increased release time for teachers to plan and carry out lessons; such collaboration was a regular component of faculty development.

The principal supported the focus of the National Centre for Excellence in the Teaching of Mathematics (NCETM) in Great Britain, which calls for teachers to "have easy access to high quality, evidence-based, maths-specific, continuing, professional development (CPD) at every point of their career." The principal also supports a mentor for new faculty during their first year who meet weekly with new teachers.

Hallmarks of This Mathematics Department

Teacher collaboration is considered as a key to allowing mathematics teachers to transition from a more procedural, pedagogical approach to one that is focused on a real-life, problem-based conceptual approach. This major change in teaching approach is a big ask for mathematics teachers worldwide. Leadership in Ireland recognized the need for teacher collaboration after their three-year rollout of a more conceptual approach and pivoted to the Japanese lesson study approach where faculty plan and execute lessons together. Observation of two Algebra II courses back-to-back taught by different teachers demonstrated the extent of the joint development of lessons.

The two observed courses illustrated the benefits of such collaboration: the starters (anticipatory set or bell ringer) were extremely well designed. They integrated two possible standardized test questions: a question for review of the previous day's work, and a question to assess readiness for the current lesson. Student engagement and participation epitomized the rest of the lesson as students grappled with real-life conceptual issues.

Students performed in a supportive atmosphere that had an air of pride in the knowledge that, while they often struggled with the content, they were some of the best and brightest students who often excel at mathematics. The dividends for their hard work would be substantial. Previous student success affirmed that they would succeed and that the future was bright.

Observing a mathematics department meeting after school the day of the visit verified the focus on pedagogical questions that was distinctive. This visit reinforced the importance of real change occurring at the local school level. Teachers need support and encouragement from direct supervisors if they are expected to take on the enormous task of teaching more conceptually. The lessons mimicked Margaret Smith and Mary Stein's (2011) focus on basics of class discussion: (a) anticipating, (b) monitoring, (c) selecting, (d) sequencing, and (d) connecting.

Observation of classes confirmed that the passion and enthusiasm of the seven mathematics teachers were commendable. The majority of problems addressed in the classroom were appropriate for group work discussion after students individually considered options. Problems were carefully selected through the process of faculty discussion and were real-life oriented. Good lesson planning gave way to great lesson designs.

The environment was clearly a safe environment where mistakes were simply stepping-stones for clearer understanding. Teachers encouraged and supported hard work and good attempts at comprehension. The prevailing teacher attitude was that the closer one's relationship to students the harder they worked to succeed.

The formal homework approach, done every two weeks, provided a way for teachers to individually assess each student and provide regular, significant feedback on student understanding. Faculty development occurred after school on a regular basis. Teachers emphasized techniques focused on excellent questioning approaches. Building close teacher/student relationships was frequently discussed in the faculty interview portion of the research. For communication purposes teachers use a traffic-light model (red light, yellow light, green light) to assess understanding from the student perspective.

An asserted effort was described by the department chair focused on a unified language used throughout the school system to help clarify mathematical terms. A questioning emphasis was apparent. Teachers were always asking clarifying questions of students. The commitment of all teachers to continue to learn and grow as mathematics teachers was inspiring.

Students notice when they see your effort to learn and improve your teaching. Taking a research-based approach to school improvement is championed by Coalition for Evidence-Based Education (CEBE), which advocates for finding research evidence, evaluating, translating, and then sharing it. Working this process with the assistance of higher education professionals holds out hope for everyone who entered the teaching profession seeking to make a difference.

MODEL SCHOOL IN JAPAN

Another exemplary school that participated in this research project is located in Tokyo, Japan. The school was the alma mater of the translator used during the visit to the schools in the area. The translator informed the researcher that it was not the kind of school that would provide keen insights into a conceptual approach to learning, since her experience ten years earlier was a lecture approach where faculty stand on a raised lecture platform and instruct students who diligently take notes. Both the researcher and the translator were surprised, observing mathematics teachers walking around the room overseeing small-group discussions and soliciting feedback from students all around the classroom.

Things had changed in the ten years since the translator attended school there. The government wants students to help each other. Students working in groups is now more valued than great orators sharing insights and students taking notes. Yet change comes hard. Schools in Japan, like elsewhere around the world, have been slow to adapt to the prescribed changes. This school had transitioned from a school with an excellent reputation for being successful in athletics to a school known for high academic achievement.

The schools' students now were admitted to the most prestigious universities in Japan and Europe on a regular basis. Observations of mathematics classrooms confirmed that student engagement and group work are major emphases. How had this principal succeeded in changing such an embedded culture while so many others fall short?

The interpreter noted that the current principal, who had worked diligently to guide the new approach, had been her high school history teacher. The emphasis to teach mathematics more conceptually with the goal of preparing students for more advanced mathematics courses was indeed a nationwide initiative. However other schools visited appeared much less settled in the process of adapting to these new approaches. One school observed was just beginning to focus on this issue, despite the nationwide focus for the past five years. Why do some schools excel at change while others struggle?

Impact of National Change Focus

While most schools in Japan, like those around the world, have been slow to accept the new pedagogical approach focused on an emphasis in real-world problems that engages students daily in productive struggle, this principal got on board early. To be fair, the approach seems counterintuitive: take students who are struggling with the challenges of learning mathematics and have them grapple with more conceptual ideas instead of simply memorizing facts and trust that they will enjoy the challenge and continue to take more difficult upper-level courses. This principal was an early convert to this approach. Numerous students have benefited from his foresight.

A little context might be helpful. Most mathematics classrooms in Japan have approximately forty students in the class. The Tokyo school system will provide an extra mathematics teacher if teachers agree to focus on the new approaches geared to student collaboration as they attempt more real-life problems. This focus, what NCTM refers to as productive struggle, is prevalent in Japanese schools now. This principal believed that making such a transition in their teaching approach would be difficult. However, with teacher collaboration and focused faculty development, changes could be accomplished.

In support of the changes, the Tokyo school system provided three years of faculty development. Teachers in Japan are hired year-round. Teachers spend much of the summer focused on remediating struggling students and in faculty development. Each month in the summer is set aside for faculty development and growth. Teachers have an action plan of improvement each year. Even well-established teachers are looking to improve. This principal was actively discussing teaching approaches and observing classrooms.

The other big story in Japan is that it is estimated that more than 70 percent of students have a tutor each evening who helps them with mathematics understanding. This frees mathematics teachers to focus on more conceptual ideas during the classroom. This provides for a structure something similar to flipping the classroom so classroom time can focus on productive struggle with teacher guidance.

New teacher training is extensive in Japan, lasting a full three years for novice teachers. All teachers in the model school collaborate on lessons at least once weekly. Younger teachers are sometimes paired with more experienced teachers for collaborative work. Every year every mathematics teacher in Japan has two full-day sessions on how to teach more conceptually. Teachers attempt to tie mathematics to the sciences for special emphasis.

Game Plan of Local Principal Revealed

So how had this principal succeeded when so many other leaders come up short? An interview revealed his belief in and commitment to his local teachers. He had faith that encouraging and fully supporting teacher dialogue and collaboration along with a shift from lecture to student engagement would make a difference. He established a culture where it was okay to help each other learn and grow. The principal generates data and sits with each teacher to discuss ramifications of the data.

He invested time and personal support in helping mathematics teachers step down off their platform and walk around the classroom guiding student learning. Teachers made it their focus to help students move the discussion forward to progress, not just emphasizing student effort. Results mattered, not just effort. Teachers were encouraged to be upbeat and positive. They were encouraged to expose their passion for the topic.

Teachers were encouraged to incorporate humor and an upbeat attitude in addition to the high expectations. At one school teachers were observed giving high fives to students in the hallway. One teacher emphatically noted that good relationships are important when you have high expectations for students.

Teachers frequently assessed student understanding throughout the lesson and adjusted their teaching accordingly. A teacher created a black box (function machine) where students would drop a ball at the top and out would come an answer at the bottom. It was an ingenious manipulative to help students understand functions. Teachers looked for ways to help students discover and uncover the mysteries of mathematics. Brighter students always seek extra help. Sometimes the teacher must reach out to other students who do not ask for help. Awareness and empathy are key.

High expectations were predominant. Classes are required to be fifty-minute sessions and no less. This school asked special permission for sixty-five-minute mathematics classrooms while they seek to teach more conceptually. A one-year exemption was approved. At the school, students are provided three hundred questions aligned to the national test. Students work on those throughout the school year in preparation for their standardized test. Assessments were considered valuable tools to evaluate attainment of desired outcomes. They were not viewed as arbitrary hurdles to limit learning or goals unto themselves. This school also has developed collaborative partnerships with another school.

Active learning is a targeted goal. Pair-and-share along with group work is a common approach observed in Japanese classrooms. Student dialogue is a goal. When asked how their principal could help, the teachers frequently mentioned the need for more time to plan, more time to collaborate, and fewer students in class. Success overcomes stress when helping students learn and grow. Building personal relationships with students was an emphasis. Teachers mentioned the importance of providing help sessions at least once a week.

Some teachers form study groups with other teachers to focus on improving their teaching. Finally the principal noted that it makes no sense to tell teachers to improve with mere words while they are being trained to help students understand big ideas. In the same way that we urge students to explore different approaches, we want teachers to explore different approaches and choose what works best for them.

This school also utilizes a Lesson Study approach, which was developed by the Japanese. That process has been spread all around the world, including training seminars in Chicago. The approach involves faculty designing a lesson together with the assistance of a university professor, or other expert, and then executing the lesson delivery with four or five teachers assessing student comprehension. The follow-up meeting provides dialogue on how the teaching approach succeeded and how plans should be adjusted for future lessons.

MODEL SCHOOL IN SOUTH KOREA

The final exemplary school used in this chapter is a school that agreed to participate in this research project located in Seoul, South Korea. Their first comments were to express surprise that someone from the United States would visit seeking ideas from them. The principal noted that they feel they are ten years behind other countries in focusing on exploring ways to teach more conceptually. One focus they embrace is the need for all teachers to constantly be learning and growing.

The principal noted that mathematics teachers often observe each. He encourages collaboration and provides the support needed to help make it happen. Teachers are not shy about observing each other and being observed. This principal provides opportunities to observe teachers in other disciplines if that helps the teacher.

A focus that the principal shared involves the use of technology. The school encourage teachers to use technology in lessons and in preparation for the next day's session. Students observe video clips in preparation for the next day's lesson. It was noted that students work in groups and then present their conclusions in front of the class. After presentations the entire class applauded. The teacher portrayed a very positive demeanor, with passion and enthusiasm prevalent and evident.

Class sizes ranged from thirty to thirty-five. There was a focus on problem-based learning. One teacher noted that students do not hate mathematics, they hate mathematics teachers. Therefore teachers work on engaging students and exciting them about grappling with upper levels of mathematics understanding. One teacher posited that positive relationships with students are vital if we are to motivate more to choose STEM careers.

Mathematics teachers described an extensive framework for teacher collaboration, joint lesson planning, and observations. They noted no one is shy about observing others teach. Group work is a major emphasis. Technology is considered a positive motivator for students. Audio, video, television, and snazzy PowerPoints are prevalent. Student can access preview material each night before the lesson. Numerous teachers mentioned that technology can be very motivating. Collaboration extends to interaction with other schools. One teacher involved in an interview explained that he was observing a faculty member from another school.

Teachers described the government's emphasis on effective teaching of mathematics. Some of the teachers noted how the government sent them to Australia to learn more about teaching with productive struggle. One teacher explained that teaching is the second most coveted job position in the country next to government work. In fact only the top 10 percent of students are accepted into education departments. Respect for teachers and their pay have risen considerably. Parents are convinced, as are students, that education is the key to future prosperity and happiness.

Teachers believe it's their job to find ways to intrigue their students. Good teachers have a force of energy regarding the teaching of mathematics. Therefore it is important to have a personal knowledge and connection with their students. In an effort to adjust the curriculum to be more conceptually based, the government is in the process of trimming down the amount of work so that what is taught can be done from a problem-based, productive struggle approach. A teacher noted that 80 percent of students have tutors each evening. The principal mentioned the need to adjust the budget to include even more use of technology and collaboration, within the school and with other schools. Principals must give authority back to teachers to allow them to adjust.

SUMMARY

Teachers in schools visited in Europe and Asia have been incentivized to make significant changes in their teaching approach. This has been accomplished through efforts of principals who recognized the enormity of the change that was needed. These principals provided moral and financial support, allowing teachers to have extended time in class to challenge students to undertake the demanding approach focused on conceptual understanding.

These teachers demonstrated a real propensity to collaborate in an effort to better engage their students. The vibrant atmosphere provided a place of learning and growth to which schools in the United States have long aspired. As one student put it, "Good teachers have a real force of energy regarding the subject of mathematics."

Chapter Ten

Rigor Requires Relationships

James Freemyer

PRE-READING REFLECTION

1. Mathematics teachers traditionally have focused more on content than relationships with students. Why are things different now?
2. Why do better relationships with students transform into better student performance?
3. What can mathematics teachers do to motivate more students to choose STEM careers?
4. How does one build better student relationships with all students?
5. Why are initial contacts with students so very important?

WHAT TO EXPECT IN THIS CHAPTER

Courses that require academic rigor necessitate the extensive pursuit of radically positive engagement with equal fervor. Much like loving and playing with a child positions a parent to discipline and correct, student support and engagement enables faculty to promote productive struggle. Asking students who have had poor experiences in their study of mathematics to attempt a new approach which requires much more effort on their part is a big ask.

It almost seems counterproductive to have as your goal motivating more students to pursue advanced mathematics courses while simultaneously increasing the required effort necessary to succeed. When this occurs in conjunction with personal connection and increased student engagement, students gladly jump on board. One South Korean teacher noted that good teachers have a *force of energy* regarding mathematics.

TEACHING MORE CONCEPTUALLY

Classrooms in Europe and Asia verified that this approach to increased faculty/student relationships is not only possible but it is exactly what students seek. A connection with an admired adult who invests time and effort into a young person's life is not only possible but probable when faculty go the extra mile to bond with and encourage their students. Many mathematics teachers can point back to special teachers who excited them and whose personal connection ignited a deep desire to learn more.

One transforming mathematics teacher from years ago was Sister Mary Karlanne. Students remember sitting in her algebra class expecting to hate mathematics and discovering it was interesting, bordering on exciting. It gave them a personal connection with a much-respected teacher who knew how to engage students in thought-provoking ideas that help operate and explain the workings of the universe.

The beauty and significance of mathematical content sparked student imagination as they sought to understand the world. She made students excited to learn. She engaged the class not with inspiring lectures, but with sound pedagogy that put the onus on students to seek to understand as she patiently nudged the entire class to deeper understanding. Her role in the classroom was not to judge the correctness of answers but to guide the class along a path of learning that makes deep understanding not only possible but probable.

She built meaningful relationships with students that changed their lives. Once students had her in class they wanted her for future classes. Other mathematics teachers paled in comparison. As Billy Graham said: "It is the Holy Spirit's job to convict, God's job to judge, and my job to love." The same is true for math teachers. Standardized testing will convict, grades will judge, but the teacher's job is to love like so many effective mathematics teachers do.

Marzano, Pickering, and Heflebower (2011) described the needed change in approach as utilizing "cognitively complex tasks with real-world applications" (p. 14). He noted that when students are expected to merely regurgitate information, they often fail to see the material's relevance. However, when students are challenged to use ideas to "solve problems, make decisions, conduct investigations, and create hypotheses regarding real-world issues, they are more likely to see what they are learning as important" (Marzano, 2011, p. 14). I experienced this sense of exploration in classroom after classroom in the exemplar school Scotland. It can be done. The more we help our students succeed, the more we truly love them.

Can Transformational Leadership Inform Teacher Practice?

The focus of transformational leadership could help inform our teaching approach as it relates to working with young people. Transformational leadership is a leadership approach often considered by people in the education field. Can its principles also inform teacher practices? Transformation leadership serves as a theoretical basis for the call for teachers to inspire their students through intentional relationships.

Transformational leadership is divided into four components on which leadership practice hopes to focus. The first component is idealized influence, where the leader attempts to provoke strong emotions and build respect in the follower (Menaker and Bahn, 2008, p. 984). The followers identify and emulate a leader's behaviors, standards, and conduct. In other words, the leader motivates students by portraying a passion for the subject.

No longer is it acceptable to admit that mathematics is boring but really smart people can do it. Teachers focus on exciting students to excel. Enthusiasm goes a long way. Describing how much you love what you do when coupled with providing students with the time and opportunity to grapple with the key issues cannot be overstated.

Schools observed in Europe and Asia already understand the importance of strong relationships. In Great Britain, teachers of mathematics were held in high esteem in many of the schools that were observed. This could be seen as students entered the classroom. They expressed a fondness for the teachers. When teachers were asked, they acknowledged it, describing the importance of extra efforts to help students as a key to such a positive mathematics culture. Teachers shared their efforts to help students in class, after school, and on Saturdays. Individual assessments, positive encouragement, and gentle nudging provided an atmosphere of appreciation and concern. One teacher in Scotland said good relationships with students were the real key to having an impact.

Schools in Ireland have achieved this positive, cultural atmosphere through years of success that followed inspiring students to expend extra effort to succeed. It was not just the teachers selling the benefits of understanding advanced coursework. The federal government made success in mathematics an extra bump in acceptance into preferred universities. Mathematics teachers in Ireland tap into that special sentiment that mathematics people can expect success in life. Students who experience any success are made to feel special.

Schools in both Japan and South Korea morphed from a culture of lecture and note-taking to a culture focused on conceptual understanding. Mathematics teachers spend considerable time after school and on Saturdays helping students understand the current classroom topic as well as the list of possible problems from past standardized tests. Students who took upper-level mathematics courses were encouraged to have very positive feelings about their accomplishments.

The second component of transformational leadership is termed individualized consideration, whereby leaders provide support, encouragement, and personal development. This cannot be overstated. Teachers would "spend time teaching and coaching, treating others as individuals, considering each individual's needs, abilities, and aspirations, while developing their strengths" (Menaker and Bahn, 2008, p. 984). In this context it would entail finding ways to assist all students as they seek to grow in their understanding of mathematics.

In Europe and Asia, teachers rotated taking time during lunch, before school, or after school to assist students. One school in Scotland described the current reality where more than twenty students come in each Saturday to prepare for standardized tests and weekly assignments. A school in Japan provided students with a long list of problems that may appear on the standardized test and on which they work week by week. When students experience situations where teachers demonstrate help above and beyond the norm, it usually increases student efforts.

A little teacher help and some personal success ignite student determination to succeed. When students experience success, they become more motivated to keep improving. Teachers in England rotating at Saturday help sessions generate increased student effort. Delegating the work to students while causing them to grapple with key concepts dramatically increases student participation and enhanced understanding.

The third component of transformational leadership is intellectual stimulation, where teachers "reexamines critical assumptions, seek differing perspectives, examines problems, and suggests novel ways to complete assignments" (Menaker and Bahn, 2008, p. 984). Real-world problems coupled with extra time to grapple with the big issues help students individually and in groups to learn on their own. Understanding these concepts simply requires time. Principals can build sufficient time into the schedule for students to work on complex questions. Teachers can nudge and guide students to obtain a better grasp of complex ideas. Working as partners with faculty in the science department help students realize it's about them personally, not just math.

Finally, transformational leadership's fourth component involves inspirational motivation. This involves the teacher being enthusiastic about accomplishments, "a vision for the future, and confidence in goals" (Menaker and Bahn, 2008, p. 984). Teachers can inspire students by wearing their passion on their sleeves. Teachers in Japan got excited

Figure 10.1. Rigor requires relationship. *Credit:* Nathan Freemyer, graphic artist.

about student learning and growth even to the point of high fives in the hallway. See figure 10.1. Students need to know and understand that teaching this course is what I love to do. Tackling a challenging problem and experiencing enough success to warrant celebration provides an intellectual rush not easily duplicated. High-tech companies can provide a model for engendering an overall excitement for student success.

Why Extra Assistance Builds Better Relationships

A key component of motivating young people to consider additional courses in any field involves providing extra assistance. When a teacher, any teacher, communicates a commitment to assist students above and beyond what can normally be expected, it provides an emotional boost that is significant. When a school department provides a helping, nurturing atmosphere, students often respond with a reciprocal effort. Schools observed in Europe and in Asia that had the most success on standardized tests all focused on extra help. Yet mathematics teachers have not been characterized as being sympathetic to individual student achievement, particularly when students are only average in ability.

Providing extra assistance should include time in class for teachers to walk around and nudge students forward in their quest to understand complex ideas. This becomes more important as teachers raise the conceptual expectations for mathematics understanding. Time for group discussion, coupled with teacher encouragement, builds meaningful relationships with students that can translate into positive motivation.

The biggest surprise from this research in Europe and Asia was the necessity of extra help for students and the extent that teachers provided the assistance willingly. Outside-of-class assistance included regularly scheduled help time, lunch help sessions, after-school gatherings, and even Saturday-morning sessions. Teachers even provided help videos for students to review in advance of a challenging subject.

Interviews with academic leaders made it clear that extra help was a joint responsibility between school leadership and local mathematics teachers. Building student help sessions into a teacher's schedule was a joint venture between principals and teachers. Teachers should not be expected to bear the weight of extra assistance alone. In Asia that was made more doable with larger class sizes. Should teachers be given help and a voice in designing workload schedules that allow for more student assistance? Does this become more important as course cognitive expectations become more demanding?

Extra help correlates directly with significant relationships. More than 50 percent of teachers interviewed mentioned the importance of student/teacher relationships early in the interview sessions. Observations in the classrooms of highly successful mathematics departments demonstrated a strong connection between academic success and emphasis on student/teacher relationships.

Relationship Emphasis in Asia

One teacher in South Korea noted that without relationships there is no good way to teach mathematics. Teachers in one South Korean school provide help sessions every day between 3 and 6 p.m. Teachers were quick to incorporate technology into helping students comprehend challenging concepts. One South Korean teacher described how student happiness is a top priority. Student interest and confidence are at an all-time high.

Stereotypical ideas about Asian mathematics teachers being aloof or unapproachable were shattered during my visit. Every teacher worked to engage and assist students in the pursuit of success. A total of 70 percent of teachers interviewed mentioned the importance of building relationships with students. Teachers realized that their extra efforts often result in extra efforts from students.

Collaboration Builds Excitement

Teachers who are open to new ideas send a powerful message to students that mathematics is important. In South Korea, teachers regularly visit other schools in the quest to improve. This sends a clear message to students that teachers would do anything to help students succeed. That sparks a culture of achievement. In South Korea, new teachers receive sixty hours of training annually during their first three years of teaching. Master teachers arrange weekly sessions of teacher collaboration. One teacher confirmed, "mathematics teachers observe each other a lot."

Teachers understand the challenge of teaching with a problem-based approach. Collaboration with STEM colleagues is extensive. Teachers in

South Korea shared that students do not hate mathematics, just mathematics teachers, particularly ones who fail to ignite a spark in students. Teachers frequently provide preview materials for students the night before it is introduced.

Principals find ways to provide collaboration time among mathematics teachers within the school and with other schools. The focus is on higher-order thinking. The commitment to learn and grow was so strong that the government provided funds for teachers to go to Australia for special training. When teachers collaborate with other mathematics teachers, it fans the flame of excitement and enthusiasm that impacts every student.

SUMMARY

Effective mathematics teachers can no longer provide methodical lectures devoid of feeling and excitement and expect to excite dreams in the hearts of students. Our best and brightest students have long understood the wonder of learning as they realize that it is within their grasp to accomplish something special with their lives. These bright students understood the opportunities that awaited them. When will average and below-average students experience this same excitement as they realize that they too can reach new heights? A solid understanding of mathematics and STEM courses can open up great opportunities for all students. This will occur only if principals are willing to invest support, time, and finances to ensure a better future for all.

Chapter Eleven

Scenario: Down in the Trenches

Rocky Wallace

COLLABORATION

Mark Anderson was beginning his third year as principal of Martin High School and was depressed over the ongoing low performance of his students in STEM courses—especially math. As he looked at the conference breakout sessions, he wandered over to the presentation next to the large ballroom where lunch would be served. He had brought his family with him to this annual summer education conference and was looking forward to an evening of leisure at a local amusement park.

"Hey, Mark, how's it going, young man?"

Mark looked around and there stood his former principal from when he was in high school. "Well, one of my all-time favorite people . . . Mrs. Weathers, how are you doing?"

"Oh, trying to be a superintendent. Miss my high school back home. I had heard you were now in administration, Mark. How do you like it?"

"To be honest, it's not a bad gig. I love helping the staff and connecting with parents and interacting with the kids. But I need some help with how to improve our student achievement in the sciences, especially in math."

"Well, son, fret no more. Join me in this session on effective collaboration. I heard these folks present last summer, and this model is changing my district."

"Really? OK, I'm in. Let's go."

In the next hour, Mark sat mesmerized as teachers, students, parents, and administrators shared example after example of how the twenty-first-century classroom and a new paradigm in how to do "school" had transformed an entire school community.

And he scribbled on the front of his conference guide: "This would transform Martin High School as well. Must do it! But how?"

On the drive home later that week, Mark went through each person on his staff in his mind, visualizing what their classroom would be like if they adopted the approach he had seen illustrated at the conference. Two names surfaced. "My two experienced teachers in the math department. They have a lot of influence on the others on their team. I truly believe they would embrace this. But I will have to reprioritize my time to lend support as never before."

Mark didn't waste any time. "Well, I know you're wondering why I called you two into the office on a Monday morning in the middle of summer break."

"Yea, is kind of weird, Mr. Anderson. What's up?" Julie smiled, as she figured she and Kate were going to be given a project of some kind.

"Have you ever heard of a program called, 'Learning Together—Re-thinking How to Create a STEM Friendly School'?"

Both teachers looked at each other and laughed. "We were just discussing this last week Mr. Anderson!" Kate couldn't contain her excitement as she went on to explain the school visit she and Julie had made a couple of months earlier to observe the most successful math program in the region.

"So, can it work here?" Mark knew the answer, but wanted to hear Kate and Julie join in his own anticipation for what this could mean to Martin High School.

His two innovative teachers mapped out a plan that made Mark want to call his entire staff in the very next day, as they took turns articulating what they had learned on their school visit.

"Starts with initial training—one half day—for all staff."

"Then you select the small group of teachers who will do the pilot and share in detail how you are going to support this model."

"And teachers hearing what the school leadership is willing to do is critical! Mr. Anderson, your working with the department chair to provide additional time for teachers to truly implement this model would be great."

"A trainer comes in about once a month to spend the day coaching your collaborative team. This part is crucial. Has to be at least three on the team, and they must work together in rolling the program out and helping others on staff to learn how it works. Thus, teachers can truly work on new teaching approaches and obtain feedback from colleagues as they explore."

"From a student's perspective, how *does* it work?" Mark was mulling over in his mind how fast he could implement such a pilot.

"They work on real-life, challenging problems that help them gain a better conceptual understanding of key mathematics principles. Students from schools that are already using this approach describe how they prefer to be engaged instead of just being bored by taking notes and doing lots of worksheets.

"And, a more collaborative approach allows teachers to better engage students with strategies where teachers are often not as familiar. Some approaches, like a flipped classroom, involve providing videos of teacher lessons which students watch at home.

"Then during class the next day teachers serve as the 'guide on the side' as they work with students in turning the traditional classroom into more of a 'think tank' center, or a discovery lab. Lots of 'one to one' and small group coaching and exploring together. The kids love it, and the teachers do, too."

Mark smiled. "Yes, indeed. I attended a presentation on this model last week, and the students were so passionate in explaining how much more they were learning, and also helping each other."

Mark thought back to his own experiences in the old classroom model of lecture, worksheets, hard-to-understand homework, and quizzes. He had learned to play the game, but had been bored with a lot of it, and had been happy with Bs as he did not understand nearly as much as he needed to.

"And Mr. Anderson, the kids love how the model utilizes technology and essentially makes math more relevant. Thus, they're interested. They begin to realize this is a life skill that is not something to fear. Instead, it's a part of learning that can be embraced.

"But, the key is *you*. For this to work, our math department will need more planning time as well as increased time to collab together, adequate training and coaching, time to experiment and visit each other's classrooms so we can learn from each other, and thus part-time substitute teachers who have math backgrounds to allow us the needed release time. This is a change in paradigm in how to be effective in helping *all* of our students to succeed in math. Without you down in the trenches with us—guiding, supporting, providing what we need—this model will not work. It's radically different from what we have been doing."

"I get it, and I agree. I will do whatever it takes from my end. You have made my day. Will you help me share this with the faculty later this summer, and help us explore a pilot this coming fall?"

Both teachers looked at each other, grinned, and in unison exclaimed, "Yes!"

RELATIONSHIP

When Bill glanced at his schedule for fall term, he felt the butterflies return to his stomach. He had not had these since the end of spring semester. He had been assigned to Ms. Kate Harting for his junior year advanced math class. She was highly thought of in the math department at Martin High School. He had heard she was hard.

"Just what I don't need," Bill mumbled to himself, as he thought back to his sophomore year and the nightmare he had experienced in Algebra II. He had goofed off the first six weeks, and never recovered. What had formerly been all As and Bs throughout his school career had plummeted to Cs and Ds in that course, and lower grades in some other classes too. His self-confidence about school had hit rock bottom.

His mom and dad were shocked and confused and sat him down at the beginning of summer with this simple admonition: "Do your best. Whatever it was that made this past year such a struggle, let's move on. Learn from it. Grow from it. But for goodness' sake, Son, try!"

On the first day of school, Bill braced for the dreaded math class . . . fifth period, after lunch. His morning went fine, and he did indeed notice within himself a renewed commitment to pay attention, and to set goals in each class for how to get off to a good start—like he used to do in elementary and middle school.

But this class, which would review Algebra I and II, then jump into geometry and trigonometry, had him wishing he could drop the course before it started. Why did he even have to take it? He wasn't planning on majoring in math in college (if he even made it to college).

"Good afternoon, everyone. I am Ms. Kate Harting. So glad to be working alongside you this school year as we explore, and learn together, more about the fascinating world of mathematics."

Bill was pleasantly surprised. Ms. Harting's demeanor was not as autocratic as he was used to in most classes, and her inviting approach to this course was nonthreatening and actually piqued his interest a little.

"Before the hour is up, I want to show you a new way to think about how you use your mathematical abilities every day of your life in some way."

"This is strange," Bill thought to himself. "I am actually curious as to what math revelations she is going to share later on. This class, so far, is interesting. I'm not nervous. But I bet her assignments for the rest of the week will be killers! She's just reeling us in. I bet she's not this interesting and caring every day."

"Ms. Harting, give us the bottom line . . . How can we 'ace' this course?" Melissa had kept quiet as long as she could. She was one of the most popular in the junior class, and never hesitated to find out about the details.

"Good question, Melissa." Ms. Harting smiled and did not seem to have an intimidating bone in her body. Bill was impressed that she knew everyone's name already—as if she had taken the extra time to study the roster and learn them over the summer.

"Well, thanks to our principal, Mr. Anderson, we decided to develop a new model for teaching and learning math this year. I want you to experience this year in this room, and in some other venues we're going to explore, as being in 'math camp.' I want you to seize the opportunity, to dive into it, and to come out of it with a new appreciation for math as a life skill, and an open door to so, so many exciting career choices."

"Will we have homework every night? Are your tests hard?" Melissa probed.

"Our work will vary. I will be mentoring you every day, often in pairs and small groups, and we'll be doing some very interesting stuff. Mrs. Julie Roberts from across the hall will be in here working with us too, as well as our instructional assistants, from time to time. Sometimes, we'll need you to follow up outside of class . . . I will be assessing your work all the time—for each of you—sort of like a basketball coach does every day of practice.

"So, no need to fear when I assign everyone a measurement, or assessment as we call it, of some kind. It will flow right along with what we are doing every day. And often, I will assign these to individuals instead of the whole group—helping me to stay on top of your progress. This process of meeting each of you where you are at is called *differentiation*, and it is crucial if we are to have changed the typical results for each of you when end of year rolls around."

"What kind of tests do you give? I really messed up last year in Algebra II and it all started with the first exam. I failed it, and the rest of the year, I struggled." Bill couldn't believe he had blurted out a question, and then explained it, on the first day! He hated to talk in front of classmates at school.

"Bill, good news. I have every confidence that if you focus in here every day, you won't be failing exams. For example, I'm going to be nudging you along, providing individual feedback regularly—with extensive written feedback on your larger assignments every two weeks, and extra help before exams. And when you still need more time for tutoring, we'll work that in before or after school, or during lunch if necessary." Bill tried to hide his smile, but inside, he was so encouraged.

"Also, we're going to provide a Saturday-morning session for those who need it, as well as access in the evenings by phone or online for troubleshooting when you are stumped with a problem. Your math teachers in this pilot have made the commitment to be supportive in any way we can—to go the extra mile. We want all of you to succeed and grasp the concepts. Doesn't do us any good if you're struggling in our classes."

The class responded with handclaps and heads nodding.

"But the other part is I *am* going to push you—just like your basketball coach. But you will come to thirst for it, even in advanced math . . . Believe it or not."

Bill had always hated math. But, ironically, he already liked this teacher and this class. And as she began her math journey with this small cohort of high school juniors that afternoon, he listened, was engaged, and understood what she was explaining on the board. In her illustrations, she was referring to carpenters, mechanics, farmers, accountants, engineers, graphic designers, composers, doctors, technology consultants—and how they all used math skills in their daily work. It was as if Bill had had an epiphany of some kind.

REMOVING BARRIERS TO STUDENT LEARNING

Jan was glad to see her "lunch bunch" crew after returning from fall break. This was her support group, and the five freshmen had been enjoying each other's noontime wit for a while now.

"So, Jan, how's it going in math?" Wes loved to tease and knew no one in the group had done well in the first half of the semester in Mrs. Dixon's class.

"Oh, I'm lovin' it, Wes." Jan made a fake smile and everyone laughed.

"Seems to me it's the same ol' routine," Carol added. "Seems like for as long as I can remember, there are a few 'pets' that hoard the spotlight, get most of the teacher's attention, and make the top grades . . . Math seems to come so easy for them. It gets old."

"I agree." Megan was the quietest of the group, so everyone was surprised she jumped into the conversation so quickly. "I get tired of doing my best, and then being made to feel like I'm just not as smart as the straight A group."

Antonio muttered in a low voice: "It's always that way. It's just how studying math seems to be—at least in this class. I would love to spend more time learning how math relates to the real world. When we do that, and it's not very often, I do so much better . . . I get it when it relates."

"Well, I guess I opened up a can of worms." Wes looked toward Jan. "What would you do different if you could have a chat with Mrs. Dixon?"

Jan thought for a moment, then stared across the lunch room to the clock, and the TV screen students could watch during lunch . . . then looked all around the room. "See those two types of communication on the wall? Is the clock's way of telling us time better or worse than how the TV gives us information?"

"No. They're just different." Wes started to smile as he knew where Jan was going with this.

"And see all these students in here with us? They're all different. *We're* all different—unique. I'd love to see math class taught to help us learn from our own uniqueness. That's what I'd share with Mrs. Dixon . . . Why can't we receive help where we are at rather than where the A students are?"

Antonio jumped in with an example. "Like my sister and me. She reads constantly. It's her passion . . . Me? I'm on the computer every evening exploring this and that, playing technology games, googling questions about everything I can think of."

Carol raised her voice in excitement. "Oh, I wish we'd do more 'hands on' stuff! . . . So, if in math class we were using more variety—so our personal strengths were tapped into more, just maybe math would come alive for us! Instead of the same lessons over and over, we'd be *mixing it up.*" She smiled and added: "I could get used to that. And I would work harder too."

Jan looked at Megan. "What do you think, Meg?"

Megan looked back. "I vote for you to go tell Mrs. Dixon what we've all discussed here—right now." Everyone laughed.

"Well, maybe I will." Jan looked back at the clock and the TV monitor. "Mr. Anderson has been so supportive of the math pilot we keep hearing about. And he's asked us a lot this year to share our ideas for how to improve our school . . . So, maybe I just will."

ENGAGEMENT

Mark Anderson shared with his pilot team that a parent would be observing in the morning. Julie and Kate were team teaching the freshmen math class, using the new model that had been so successful in other schools.

"Don't do anything different. Just let the normal routine flow. I'll be interested to hear what Mrs. Hatton has to say. We need lots of input from various stakeholders in this first semester, so we can make improvements as needed." Mark was anxious to share the early results of the model to other principals in the district too but wanted plenty of evidence.

Class had already begun when Mrs. Hatton walked in, and she was amazed at what was taking place. Students were engaged in small-group work all over the room. Two teachers and one teacher's assistant were moving about, interacting with students, and answering questions, coaching, complimenting the purposeful work. Students were collaboratively learning math, while also developing individually—but at a rigorous pace, not wasting time. Everyone was engaged in focused work.

"This truly is amazing." Mrs. Hatton voiced her pleasant surprise as Kate came over to chat and answer any questions.

"So this is a daily happening? This is a routine math class?"

"Yes, ma'am." Kate grinned as she enjoyed the vibes she was getting.

"How did you develop this pilot? Where did it come from?"

"Julie over there and I observed this process in another school this past spring. When Mr. Anderson came home from a summer conference raving about it, he asked us to do a trial run this first year. The plan is to implement it all over the building in the near future."

"And these kids near the wall . . . Independent work on computers . . . Remedial work?"

"Well, we don't call it that. They are going back and solving some problems they had trouble with yesterday in a group task we assigned. But we don't see it as being behind. They just need more time, that's all. See the instructional assistant over there with them? She's so good with the students. And she's great at mentoring kids in math—knows how to break it down into smaller parts. So, wow, makes such a difference."

"I don't see as many school desks as used to be the norm. But lots of tables, computer centers, and your Smart Board."

"Yea, we really don't need the rows of furniture. Too much moving around in here and working with partners. We do regularly invite folks in from various vocations to share their expertise, but the kids simply sit around the tables."

"What about textbooks? Grades? Do they cheat on tests a lot in this atmosphere?"

Just then Julie walked over to join the conversation. "Hello, so glad you came in to join us today. Textbooks? Not as often as in the past. We use a lot of online resources and websites or links, with a set of textbooks we use for specific concepts and projects . . . Grades? What you see going on right now is how they are earning their grade for this six weeks. Mastery learning. They practice, help each other, we assist as needed. It's more like a lab. They know what they need to do to succeed in this course . . . Cheating? Also rare. Certainly much less than the old 'sit and get' format. Some cheated constantly with that traditional model—sometimes out of boredom."

"And they all like this culture that combines rigor with freedom and autonomy?"

"Not just like it. They love it. Students respond better when they have to use productive struggle to understand key concepts related to mathematics. Big challenges mean significant rewards. You see, the latest research on how all our minds are so different is helping educators to reevaluate how we have traditionally done 'school.' These new findings show us that grasping math concepts is naturally going to be unique to each individual. So, we believe in diving much deeper into how each student learns, and then focusing on how to help math make sense for them."

"So, you break it all down so you're meeting each student where they are at—not just meeting the class as a whole where they are at . . . Almost how my tennis coach worked with me back in my high school days."

Kate jumped back in. "That is a good analogy. And think what all went into your own perceptions of your ability to play tennis. How your parents perceived you as an athlete, how the school valued or didn't value the tennis program, whether athletics came easy for you, the new motor skills you were developing, your muscle memory, your practice habits and whether you enjoyed practice . . . All of those variables came into play, and made a huge difference."

"Never thought of it that way," Mrs. Hatton pondered out loud.

Kate explained further. "Well, it's the same way for music, drama, or art students. But notice how their teachers have them work on their skills until they master it. And with the content areas, it's the same way too. Students often have multilayered barriers before the first day of class. Often, it's their perception that they can't do the core subjects as well—especially math and science. But we're changing that in how we explore and master math skills with this program."

A smile came over Mrs. Hatton's face. "I must say, I am impressed. I wonder, if I volunteered to come in a day a week and helped where you needed me, would that be OK? This is the most fascinating classroom I have ever seen. It just grows on you. I'd love to in some small way be a part of your pilot."

Julie and Kate smiled, and in unison said: "Of course."

CULTURE: HIGH EXPECTATIONS, CHALLENGING WORK, THE JOY OF UNDERSTANDING

Renee's daughter Tami came bursting through the door, startling her mother. "Mom, you won't believe it! I love my class schedule this year!"

"Honey, that's wonderful! You've not been this excited since you were in primary school. What's going on this year that makes it so special?"

"Oh, it's hard to explain. One class in particular is so cool . . . Mom, I couldn't believe how much *getting it* we had in math today."

"Joy in math class? Hmm, I don't remember any of that back in my day."

"Oh, Mom, you were a whiz kid. But now me, that's another story."

"Not so, Tami. You can do anything you set your mind to, kiddo. Don't you ever forget it either. Your father and I are so proud of you. . . . Tell me more."

"Well, the teacher, Mrs. Julie Roberts, explained that this new math pilot will eventually be used as a model to change how we do our classrooms all over the school. She talked about working together a lot on our classwork, and teacher presentations and lectures being on the Internet. She said that our teachers would be by our side coaching us much of the time . . . And we would be jumping into more harder stuff than in the past—but figuring it out—not giving up on it. *Mastery*, I think she called it."

Renee stood at the sink and chuckled quietly with pleasant surprise. "Well now, tell me, what else is different about math this year?"

"Oh, Mom, my math teacher, Mrs. Roberts. She is so fun to work with! She took time today to get to know all of us and spent several minutes with me discussing what I like about math courses and what I struggle with. She is a good listener—I like that. Her approach is to be by our side every step of the way. And we can schedule extra time with her for help before or after school."

"Wow, that's great. How many times last year did I hear you say you just didn't have time to learn all of the new math concepts that were covered every week?"

"Oh, Mom, Mrs. Roberts cares about *all* of us grasping the concepts well. She pushes us to ask questions and stay with it—so our work is something we truly understand."

"Won't some students take advantage of her if she comes across as too caring?"

"Nope. And I'll tell you why. Today, she was interacting with the class, had everyone engaged in what she was explaining on the board, had us working out problems in small groups at the end of class, and gave us all work to do online this evening. And she's going to be on there with us at 9 o'clock tonight for a few minutes to answer questions and illustrate a couple of things."

"I don't remember ever having a teacher make math so interesting, Tami. Sounds like she's almost become an advocate for *all* of you to master the concepts in this course. I am impressed."

"Me too, Mom. Mrs. Roberts is all about relationship and helping us succeed. When a teacher does that part, I am more than fine with the class being challenging and taking lots of time."

Tami headed up the stairs. "Well, I need to go make an entry in my journal on our conversation. Will fit perfect for what Mrs. Roberts has us doing as a weekly task."

"She has you journaling? In math class?"

"Yep. We turn them in every Friday. It's her way of knowing each of us and our ups and downs with math on a personal level."

"Never heard of that . . . But I like it."

"Oh, Mom, you will love Mrs. Roberts. Our school's open house is this Thursday, and I want you to come meet her. She's invited all of us to bring our families by. She'll have her husband and kids there too."

"Tami, catch me before I faint. You want your father and me to come to a high school open house? Honey, are you feeling ill?"

Tami and Renee both laughed, as Renee gave her daughter a big hug.

CLOSING THOUGHTS: SERVANT LEADERSHIP

As a former principal, I keenly remember the challenges my teachers faced in making math an effective, engaging learning experience for their students. And I remember over the years the high number of people of all ages who have shared with me that they were not good in math—with many sharing that their lowest scores on the ACT were in math.

I remember my high school math classes. What had been routine and fulfilling when I was in elementary and middle school became an area of lost confidence and frustration. Not until my junior year did I begin to reconnect. The teacher that year was new, and she was relational. When she slowed down and met each of us where we were at, challenged us but also let us know there was nothing to fear, the more complex concepts of geometry and trigonometry began to sink in. Hey, I could do it after all! One of the most fulfilling courses of my high school career.

So, when Dr. Jim Freemyer contacted me a couple of summers ago and asked if I would want to collaborate on a math project that he was passionate about developing, I was definitely interested. I have not regretted it. Jim has orchestrated a gem with this book. He and the other contributing authors have cited powerful research, and the probing questions from each chapter challenge the reader to not accept what has been, but instead to explore what is making a difference presently in the math classroom.

Much weighs in the balance, as the need for stronger STEM education is at a critical stage in this global culture of high tech and a shortage of proficient specialists to master the tasks and thus meet the needs of the marketplace. Enjoy this resource, and share its epiphanies with others . . . At school, at work—at home with your own children and grandkids.

The barriers addressed in this book are indeed real, but the solutions shared here are already being mastered in pockets of twenty-first-century teaching/learning around the world.

Principals, as servant leaders, your investment in supporting and inspiring transformational change in your school is the key. Caring for your school community includes equipping and empowering your staff, and giving your students the priceless gift of *productive struggle*. Go for it.

The servant-leader is servant first. It begins with the natural feeling that one wants to serve. This conscious choice brings one to aspire to lead. The best test is: do those served grow as persons: do they, while being served, become healthier, wiser, freer, more autonomous, more likely themselves to become servants? And, what is the effect on the least privileged in society; will they benefit, or, at least, not be further deprived?
—Robert Greenleaf

Bibliography

Aguilar, Elena. *The Art of Coaching: Effective Strategies for School Transformation*. San Francisco, CA: Wiley, 2013.

American Institute of Mathematics. https://aimath.org/.

Arbinger Institute. *Leadership and Self-deception: Getting out of the Box*. Oakland, CA: Berrett-Koehler Publishers, 2010.

Baddeley, Alan D. *Working Memory, Thought, and Action*. Oxford: Oxford University Press, 2007.

Barrett, Jeffrey Edward, Douglas H. Clements, and Julie Sarama. *Children's Measurement: A Longitudinal Study of Children's Knowledge and Learning of Length, Area, and Volume*. Reston, VA: National Council of Teachers of Mathematics, *Journal for Research in Mathematics Education* Monograph Number, no. 16 (2017).

Bellanca, James, Brandt, R., *21st Century Skills: Rethinking How Students Learn*. Bloomington, IN: Solution Tree Press, 2010.

Bjork, Robert A. "Memory and Metamemory Considerations in the Training of Human Beings." Edited by Janet Metcalfe and Arthur P. Shimamura. In *Metacognition: Knowing about Knowing*. Cambridge Mass: MIT Press, 1994.

Black, J. Stewart and Hal Gregersen. *It Starts with One: Changing Individuals Changes Organizations*. Upper Saddle River, NJ: Pearson, 2008.

Black, J. Stewart and Hal Gregersen. *It Starts with One: Changing Individuals Changes Organizations*. Upper Saddle River, NJ: Pearson, 2014.

Boaler, Jo. *The Elephant in the Classroom: Helping Children Survive, Achieve and Enjoy School Maths*. London: Souvenir, 2009.

Boiselle, Ellen. *Assessment of Students with Learning Difficulties in Mathematics: Applying Neuropsychological Analysis to Standardized Measures of Arithmetic Achievement*. PhD diss., Tufts University, 2007.

Boiselle, Ellen. "Assessment of learning difficulties in arithmetic: Looking beyond standard scores." *University of Lowell Annual Colloquium Journal* XIII (2008): 1–16.

Boiselle, Ellen. "Assessing learning problems in mathematics." Keynote address presented at the annual meeting of Northeast Association of Learning Specialists (NEALS), Worcester, Massachusetts, April, 2018.

Boston College, Lynch School of Education, International Study Center. Third Annual Math and Science Study. https://timssandpirls.bc.edu/timss2015/

Boston, Melissa, Melissa Boston, Frederick Dillon, Margaret S. Smith, and Stephen Miller. *Implementing Effective Mathematics Teaching Practices in Grades 9–12*. Reston, VA: National Council of Teachers of Mathematics, 2017.

Bouck, Emily C., and Mary K. Bouck. "Mathematical Problem-Solving." In *Bridging the Gap Between Arithmetic and Algebra*, edited by Bradley S. Witzel, 119–37. Arlington, VA: Council for Exceptional Children, 2016.

Brackett, Marc A. and Dena Simmons. "Emotions Matter." *Educational Leadership* 73, no. 2 (October 2015): 22–27.

Bryant, Diane P., Sun A. Kim, Paula Hartman, and Brian R. Bryant. "Standards-Based Mathematics Instruction and Teaching Middle School Students with Mathematical Disabilities." In Teaching Mathematics to Middle School Students with Learning *Difficulties*, by Marjorie Montague and Asha K. Jitendra, 7–28. New York, NY: Guilford Press, 2006.

Burns, Marilyn. "Math Reasoning Inventory." Math Reasoning Inventory. 2012. https://mathreasoninginventory.com/.

Butterworth, Brian. "Development Dyscalculia." In *Handbook of Mathematical Cognition*, edited by Jamie I.D. Campbell, 455–67. New York, NY: Psychology Press, 2005.

CAST Universal Design for Learning Guidelines version 2.2. (2018) Retrieved from http://udlguidelines.cast.org

Chen, Milton. *Education Nation: Six Leading Edges of Innovation in Our Schools*. San Francisco, CA: Jossey-Bass, 2010.

Clark, Thomas, Mike Jansen, Amanda Harsy, Dave Klanderman, Mandi Maxwell, and Sharon Robert. "Start a Math Teacher Circle: Connect K-12 Teachers with Engaging, Approachable, and Meaningful Mathematics Problems." In *Proceedings of the Association of Christians in the Mathematical Sciences* (2018): 22–29.

Clark, Thomas, Mike Janssen, Amanda Harsy, Dave Klanderman, Mandi Maxwell, Sharon Robbert. "Start a Math Circle: Connect K-12 Teachers with Engaging, Approachable, and Meaningful Mathematical Problems." Paper presented at the Association of Christians in the Mathematical Sciences Conference, Charleston, South Carolina, May 31-June2, 2017.

Clarke, David, and Hilary Hollingsworth. "Elaborating a Model of Teacher Professional Growth." *Teaching and Teacher Education* 18, no. 8 (2002): 947–67. doi:10.1016/s0742–051x(02)00053–7.

Clintondale High School. (2013). How one school turned homework on its head with 'flipped' instruction. PBS Newshour. https://www.pbs.org/newshour/education/what-does-a-flipped-classroom-look-like-2

Cochrane Collegiate Academy. (2018). Lessons from a public school turnaround. Future Ready Schools. https://futureready.org/resource/lessons-from-a-public-school-turnaround/

Cochrane Collegiate Academy. (n.d.) Lessons from a public school turnaround. Edutopia. https://www.edutopia.org/school/cochrane-collegiate-academy

Cochrane Collegiate Academy. (2018). US News and World Report. https://www.usnews.com/education/best-high-schools/north-carolina/districts/charlotte-mecklenburg-schools/cochrane-collegiate-academy-155815

Common Core State Standards Initiative. 2018. Standards for Mathematical Practice. http://www.corestandards.org/Math/Practice/ .

Common Core State Standards Initiative (CCSSI). 2010. Common Core State Standards for Mathematics. Washington, DC: National Governors Association Center for Best Practices and the Council of Chief State School Officers. http://www.corestandards.org/wp-content/uploads/Math_Standards.pdf

Csikszentmihalyi, Mihaly. "Happiness and Creativity: Going with the Flow." *The Futurist* 31, no. 5 (September/October 1997): 8. EBSCO (9710064070).

Daggett, Bill. *The Daggett System for Effective Instruction: Alignment for Student Achievement*. Rexford, NY: International Center for Leadership in Education, 2012.

Danielson, Charlotte. "Framing Discussions about Teaching." *Educational Leadership* 72, no. 7 (April 2015): 38–41.

Darling-Hammond, Linda. *Powerful Teacher Education Lessons from Exemplary Programs*. Hoboken: Wiley, 2006.

Darling-Hammond, Linda. *The Flat World and Education: How America's Commitment to Equity Will Determine Our Future*. New York: Teachers College Press, 2010.

Davidson, Patricia S. "Mathematics Learning Viewed from a Neurobiological Model for Intellectual Functioning. Final Report: Volume One," December 1, 1983. (NIH Grant NIE-G-79–0089) ERIC (ED239914).

Deal, Terrence E. and Allan A. Kennedy. *Corporate Cultures: The Rites and Rituals of Corporate Life.* Boston, MA: Addison-Wesley Publishing, 1982.

Devine, Dympna, Declan Fahie, and Deirdre Mcgillicuddy. "What Is 'good' Teaching? Teacher Beliefs and Practices about Their Teaching." *Irish Educational Studies* 32, no. 1 (2013): 83–108. doi:10.1080/03323315.2013.773228.

Dewey, John. *Democracy and Education: An Introduction to the Philosophy of Education*. New York: The Macmillan Company, 1916.

Dougherty, Barbara, Diane Pedrotty Bryant, Brian R. Bryant, and Mikyung Shin. "Helping Students With Mathematics Difficulties Understand Ratios and Proportions." *TEACHING Exceptional Children* 49, no. 2 (November 2016): 96–105. doi:10.1177/0040059916674897.

Drapeau, Patti. *Sparking Student Creativity: Practical Ways to Promote Innovative Thinking and Problem Solving*. Alexandria, VA: ASCD, 2014.

Dufour, Richard, and Robert J. Marzano. *Leaders of Learning: How District, School, and Classroom Leaders Improve Student Achievement*. Bloomington, IN: Solution Tree Press, 2011.

Dweck, Carol S. *Mindset: The New Psychology of Success*. New York: Ballantine Books, 2016.

Dweck, Carol S. *Mindset: The New Psychology of Success*. New York: Random House, 2006.

Eichhorn, Melinda (Mindy), Peter J. DiMauro, Courtney Lacson, and Barbara Dennie. "Building the Optimal Learning Environment for Mathematics." *The Mathematics Teacher* 112, no. 4 (2019): 262–67. (2019) https://www.jstor.org/stable/10.5951/mathteacher.112.4.0262

Edutopia, retrieved from https://www.edutopia.org/school/cocchrane-collegiate -academy (2011)

Federal Science Technology Engineering and Mathematics (STEM) Education 5-Year Strategic Plan, A Report from the Committee on STEM Education, National Science and Technology Council, May, 2013, Executive Office of the President

Freemyer, James. "Challenging Teachers to Embrace Global Competition: Adapting Our Approach to Mathematics Education Supported by Research-Based Approaches." Paper presented at the Association for Teacher Education in Europe Conference, Braga, Portugal, August 25–27, 2014.

Freemyer, James. "Preparing Mathematics Students to Compete in the Global Market: Lessons Learned in Indiana, Ireland, and the U.K." Paper presented at the Indiana Council of Teachers of Mathematics, Indianapolis, Indiana, November 6–7, 2016.

Freemyer, James. "Effective Mathematics Teaching: Lessons Learned from Ireland, the U.S., the U.K., Japan, and South Korea." Paper presented at the National Council of Teachers of Mathematics Conference, Washington, D.C., April 25–28, 2018.

Freemyer, James, Olivia Fitzmaurice, and Patrick Johnson. "Motivating Young People to Seek Careers in STEM: Research Conclusions from Interviews and

Observations in Ireland and the U.K." *British Society for Research into Learning Mathematics* 35, no. 1 (February, 2015).

Freemyer, James, Patrick Johnson, and Olivia Fitzmaurice. "The Dynamics of Inclusive Leadership in the Context of a Mandated National Change Institute." Paper presented at the International Leadership Association Annual Conference, Atlanta, Georgia, November 2–6, 2016.

Freemyer, James, Patrick Johnson, and Olivia Fitzmaurice. "Effective Mathematics Teaching: Lessons Learned from Ireland, the U.S., and the U.K." Paper presented at the Association of Teacher Educators in Europe Conference, Dubrovnik, Croatia, October 23–25, 2017.

Freemyer, James, Global Examples of Leadership That Promote Follower Engagement to Drive the Process of Change, ATEE Conference, Bragal, Portugal, 14—18 April, 2019

Geary, David C. "Learning Disabilities in Mathematics: Recent Advances." In *Handbook of Learning Disabilities*, edited by H. L. Swanson, Karen R. Harris, and Steve Graham, 239–55. 2nd ed. New York, NY: Guilford Press, 2013.

Geary, David C., Mary K. Hoard, Lara Nugent, and Jennifer Byrd-Craven. "Strategy Use, Long-Term Memory, and Working Memory Capacity." In *Why Is Math So Hard for Some Children? The Nature and Origins of Mathematical Learning Difficulties and Disabilities*, edited by Daniel B. Berch and Michele M.M. Mazzocco, 83–105. Baltimore, MD: Paul H. Brookes Publishing, 2007.

Gellert, Laura and Lidia Gonzalez. "Teacher Collaboration: Implications for New Mathematics Teachers." *Current Issues in Education*, 14, no. 1. Retrieved from http://cie.asu.edu/ojs/index.php/cieatasu/articles/view/

Gilber, L. & Gonzalez, L. (2011). Teacher collaboration: Implications for new mathematics teachers. Current Issues in education, 14(1). Retrieved on 7.5.2018 from http://cie.asu.edu/ojs/index.php/eieatasu/aticle/view/

Ginsburg, Herbert P. *Entering the Child's Mind: The Clinical Interview in Psychological Research and Practice.* New York, NY: Cambridge University Press, 1997.

Glickman, Carl D. *Leadership for Learning: How to Help Teachers Succeed.* Alexandria, VA: Association for Supervision and Curriculum Development, 2002.

Goddard, Yvonne, Robert J. Miller, Ross Larsen, and Roger Goddard. "Connecting Principal Leadership, Teacher Collaboration, and Student Achievement." Paper presented at the Annual Meeting of the American Educational Research Association, Denver, Colorado, April 30–May 4, 2010.

Goldsmith, Lynn, Doerr, H., and Lewis, C., "Mathematics teachers' learning: a conceptual framework and synthesis research." *Journal of Mathematics Teacher Education* 17, no. 1 (Feb. 2014): 5.

Goleman, Daniel. *Emotional Intelligence: Why It Can Matter More than IQ.* New York: Bantam Books, 2005.

Goodwin, Bryan, Gibson, T., Lewis, D., and Rouleau, K. *Unstuck: How Curiosity, Peer Coaching, and Teaming Can Change Your School.* Alexandria, VA: ASCD, 2018.

Grant, Leslie, Strong, J., Xu, X, Popp, P., Sun, Y., and Little, C. *West Meets East: Best Practices from Expert Teachers in the U.S. and China.* Alexandria, VA: ASCD, 2014.

Greenleaf, Robert K. *Servant Leadership—A Journey into the Nature of Legitimate Power and Greatness.* Mahwah: New Jersey: Paulist Press. 2002 (25th anniversary edition).

Gruenert, Steve, and Todd Whitaker. *School Culture Rewired: How to Define, Assess, and Transform It.* Alexandria, VA: ASCD, 2015.

Guerrero, Shannon. "Teacher Change and Project Mathematics: Implications and Lessons Learned." *Bulletin of the Irish Mathematical Society* 74 (Winter 2014): 27–66. EBSCO (100596942).

Hargreaves, Andy, and Michael Fullan. *Change Wars.* Bloomington, IN: Solution Tree, 2009.

Hattie, John. *Visible Learning for Teachers: Maximizing Impact on Learning.* London: Routledge, 2012.

Hennesy, Beth A. "Reward, Task Motivation, Creativity and Teaching: Towards a Cruss-Cultural Examination." *Teachers College Record* 117, no. 10 (2015). ERIC (EJ1074697).

Hilyard, Gail Young. *Importance of Trust for Developmental Mathematics Instructors in Massachusetts Community Colleges: A Study of Its Connections to Math Anxiety and Motivation.* PhD diss., 2013.

Holmes-Bernstein, Jane, and Deborah P. Waber. "Developmental Neuropyschological Assessment: The Systemic Approach." Edited by Glen B. Baker, Alan A. Boulton, and Merrill Hiscock. In *Neuromethods. Neuropsychology.* Clifton, NJ: Humana Press, 1990.

Hughes, Elizabeth M., Sarah R. Powell, and Elizabeth A. Stevens. "Supporting Clear and Concise Mathematics Language: Instead of That, Say This." *TEACHING Exceptional Children* 49, no. 1 (September 2016): 7–17. doi:10.1177/0040059916654901.

Huinker, DeAnn, and Victoria Bill. *Implementing Effective Mathematics Teaching Practices in Kindergarten-grade 5.* Reston, VA: National Council of Teachers of Mathematics, 2017.

Humphreys, Cathy, and Ruth E. Parker. *Making Number Talks Matter: Developing Mathematical Practices and Deepening Understanding, Grades 4–10.* Portsmouth, NH: Stenhouse Publishers, 2015.

Jackson, Brad, and Ken W. Parry. *A Very Short, Fairly Interesting and Reasonably Cheap Book about Studying Leadership.* 2nd ed. London: SAGE, 2011.

Jacobs, Jennifer, and Diane Yendol-Hoppey. "Supervisor Transformation within a Professional Learning Community." *Teacher Education Quarterly* 37, no. 2 (2010): 97–114. ERIC (EJ896072)

James, Mary, and Andrew Pollard. "Introduction." *Research Papers in Education* 26, no. 3 (2011): 269–73. doi:10.1080/02671522.2011.595541.

Kachur, D.S., Stout, J.A., & Edwards, C.L. (2013). *Engaging teachers in classroom walkthroughs.* ASCD, /Alexandria, VA.

Kent County Intermediate School District. http://www.kentisd.org/.

Knight, Jim. "Escape from the Zero-Learning Zone: Why Educators Frequently Turn Away from Opportunities to Learn, and What We Can Do about It." *Educational Leadership* 76, no. 3 (2018): 20–26. EBSCO (132792677)

Knowles, Malcolm S., Elwood F. Holton, and Richard A. Swanson. *The Adult Learner: The Definitive Classic in Adult Education and Human Resource Development.* London: Routledge, 2015.

Kraft, Charles H. "Culture, Worldview and Contextualization." In *Perspectives on the World Christian Movement: A Reader.* 4th ed. Pasadena, CA: William Carey Library, 2009.

Larson, Matt. "Bringing Needed Coherence and Focus to High School Mathematics." *National Council of Teachers of Mathematics.* October 25, 2016. https://www.nctm.org/News-and-Calendar/Messages-from-the-President/Archive/Matt-Larson/Bringing-Needed-Coherence-and-Focus-to-High-School-Mathematics/

Larson, Matt. "A perfect storm of data: We must take action!" *National Council of Teachers of Mathematics.* January 17, 2017. https://www.nctm.org/News-and-Calendar/Messages-from-the-President/Archive/Matt-Larson/A-Perfect-Storm-of-Data_-We-Must-Take-Action!/

Lawson, Matthew R., Francis "Skip" Fennell, Thomasenia Lott Adams, Juli K. Dixon, Beth McCord Kobett, and Jonathan A. Wray, eds. "Using High-performing Collaborative Teams for Mathematics." In *Common Core Mathematics in a PLC at Work.* Grades K-2. Bloomington, IN: Solution Tree Press, 2012.

LePage, Pamela. "Introduction." In *Preparing Teachers for a Changing World: What Teachers Should Learn and Be Able to Do,* by Linda Darling-Hammond and John Bransford, 1–39. San Francisco, CA: Jossey-Bass, 2017.

Lewis, Katherine E. "Difference Not Deficit: Reconceptualizing Mathematical Learning Disabilities." *Journal for Research in Mathematics Education* 45, no. 3 (2014): 351–96. doi:10.5951/jresematheduc.45.3.0351.

Liesveld, Rosanne, Miller, J. *Teach with Your Strengths: How Great Teachers Inspire Their Students.* New York: Gallup Press, 2005.

Lovely, Suzette, and Austin G. Buffum. *Generations at School: Building an Age-friendly Learning Community.* Thousand Oaks, CA: Corwin Press, a Sage Publications Company, 2007.

Lubienski, Sarah. "Mathematics Education and Reform in Ireland: An Outsider's Analysis of Project Maths." *Bulletin of the Irish Mathematical Society* 67 (Summer 2011): 27–55. EBSCO (67433710).

Lynch, Sararose D., Jessica H. Hunt, and Katherine E. Lewis. "Productive Struggle for All: Differentiated Instruction." *Mathematics Teaching in the Middle School* 23, no. 4 (2018): 194–201. doi:10.5951/mathteacmiddscho.23.4.0194.

Ma, Liping. *Knowing and Teaching Elementary Mathematics: Teachers' Understanding of Fundamental Mathematics in China and the United States.* Anniversary ed. New York, NY: Routledge, 2010.

Marolda, Maria R. *Mathematics Diagnostic/Prescriptive Inventory.* 2016. MS, Boston: Children's Hospital Learning Disability Program.

Marolda, Maria R., and Ellen C. Boiselle. "Mathematics Learning Profiles: Mathematics Learning Viewed from a Neuropsychological Perspective." 2018a. MS.

Marolda, Maria R., and Ellen C. Boiselle. "Differentiated Teaching Strategies." 2018b. MS.

Marolda, Maria R., and Patricia S. Davidson. "Assessing Mathematical Abilities and Learning Approaches." In *Windows of Opportunity: Mathematics for Students with Special Needs*, edited by C. A. Thornton and N. S. Bley. Reston, VA: NCTM, National Council of Teachers of Mathematics, 1994.

Marolda, Maria R., and Patricia S. Davidson. "Mathematical Learning Profiles and Differentiated Teaching Strategies." *Perspectives* 26, no. 3 (2000): 10–15.

Marzano, Robert J. "Developing Expert Teachers." In *On Excellence in Teaching.* Bloomington, IN: Solution Tree Press, 2010.

Marzano, Robert J., Debra J. Pickering, and Tammy Heflebower. *The Highly Engaged Classroom.* Bloomington, IN: Marzano Research Laboratory, 2011.

Meltzer, Lynn. *Promoting Executive Function in the Classroom.* New York: Guilford Press, 2010.

Menaker, Ronald and Rebecca S. Bahn. "How Perceived Physician Leadership Behavior Affects Physician Satisfaction." *Mayo Clinic Proceedings* 83, no. 9 (2008): 983–988. https://www.mayoclinicproceedings.org.

Montague, Marjorie. "Math Problem Solving for Upper Elementary Students with Disabilities." The Access Center. 2005. http://165.139.150.129/intervention/Math%20Problem%20Solving%20for%20Upper%20Elementary%20Students%20with%20Disabilities.pdf

Montague, Marjorie. "Self-Regulation and Mathematics Instruction." *Learning Disabilities Research & Practice* 22, no. 1 (February 1, 2007): 75–83. ERIC (EJ756848).

Montague, M. (2005). Math problem solving for upper elementary students with disabilities. Retrieved from http://165.139.150.129/intervention/Math%20 Problem%20Solving%20for%20 Primary%20Elementary%20Students%20 with%20Disabilties.pdf (2005)

Montague, Marjorie. "Self-regulation Strategies for Better Math Performance in Middle School." Edited by Marjorie Montague and Asha K. Jitendra. In *Teaching Mathematics to Middle School Students with Learning Difficulties*, 89–107. New York: Guilford Press, 2006.

Montague, Marjorie, and Samantha Dietz. "Evaluating the Evidence Base for Cognitive Strategy Instruction and Mathematical Problem Solving." *Exceptional Children* 75, no. 3 (2009): 285–302. doi:10.1177/001440290907500302.

Murrell, Peter C., Jr., Mary Diez, Sharon Felman-Nemser, and Deborah L. Schussler, eds. *Teaching as a Moral Practice: Defining, Developing, and Assessing Professional Dispositions in Teacher Education*. Cambridge, Mass: Harvard Education Press, 2010.

The National Assessment of Educational Progress. 2018. https://nces.ed.gov/ nationsreportcard.

National Center on Universal Design for Learning. 2010. "UDL: Principles and Practice" https://www.youtube.com/watch?v=pGLTJw0GSxk&t=13s

National Council of Teachers of Mathematics (NCTM) (2000). Principles and standards for school mathematics. Reston, VA: National Council of Teachers of Mathematics.

National Council of Teachers of Mathematics (NCTM) (2014). Principles to actions: Ensuring mathematical success for all. Reston, VA: National Council of Teachers of Mathematics.

Palmer, Parker J. *The Courage to Teach: Exploring the Inner Landscape of a Teacher's Life*. San Francisco: Jossey-Bass, 1998.

Palmer, Parker J. *Let Your Life Speak: Listening for the Voice of Vocation*. San Francisco: Jossey-Bass, 2000.

Parrish, Sherry D. "Number Talks Build Numerical Reasoning." *Teaching Children Mathematics* 18, no. 3 (2011): 198. doi:10.5951/teacchilmath.18.3.0198.

Parrish, Sherry. *Number Talks: Helping Children Build Mental Math and Computation Strategies, Grades K-5*. Sausalito, CA, USA: Math Solutions, 2010.

Perez, Jason. "Taking the Doors off the Classroom Through Collaboration." Hot Chalk Education Network. Accessed July 10, 2018. https://www.hotchalk educationnetwork.com/collaboration-with-purpose/.

Poulos, Jennifer. "Making Space: The Value of Teacher Collaboration." Boston, MA: Rennie Center for Education Research & Policy. (2014) http://www .renniecenter.org/sites/default/files/2017–01/EdVestors-Making-Space-The -Value-of-Teacher-Collaboration-2014.pdf.

Principles and Standards for School Mathematics: An Overview. Reston, VA: National Council of Teachers of Mathematics, 2000.

Principles to Actions: Ensuring Mathematical Success for All. Reston, VA: NCTM, National Council of Teachers of Mathematics, 2014.

Protheroe, Nancy. "Teacher Efficacy: What Is It and Does It Matter?" *Principal* 87, No. 5 (2008): 42–45. ERIC (EJ806309)

Rose, Todd. *The End of Average: How We Succeed in a World That Values Sameness.* New York: HarperCollins Publishers, 2015.

Russell, Susan Jo. "Developing Computational Fluency with Whole Numbers." *Teaching Children Mathematics* 7, no. 3 (2000): 154–58. ERIC (EJ670310).

Sanders, William, and June Rivers. *Cumulative and Residual Effect of Teachers on Future Academic Achievement.* Knoxville, TN: University of Tennessee Value-Added Research and Assessment Center, 1996.

Schein, Edgar, *Organizational Culture and Leadership,* The Jossey-Bass & Management Series, 5th Edition, 2004. ISBN 13 9978–1119212041

Schleifer, David, Chloe Rinehart, and Tess Yanisch. "Teacher Collaboration in Perspective: A Guide to Research. San Fransisco, CA: The Spencer Foundation and Public Agenda, 2017. https://www.publicagenda.org/files/Public Agenda_TeacherCollaborationInPerspective_AGuideToResearch_2017.pdf.

Schoenfeld, Alan. *How We Think. A Theory of Goal-Oriented Decision Making and Its Educational Applications.* New York: Routledge, 2011.

Schoenfeld, A. H., & the Teaching for Robust Understanding Project. (2016). An Introduction to the Teaching for Robust Understanding (TRU) Framework. Berkeley, CA: Graduate School of Education. Retrieved from http://tru framework.org or http://map.mathshell.org/trumath.php.

Schoenfeld, Alan. "The Teaching for Robust Understanding Project." An Introduction to the Teaching for Robust Understanding (TRU) Framework. https://truframework.org/.

Schuchardt, Kirsten, Claudia Maehler, and Marcus Hasselhorn. "Working Memory Deficits in Children with Specific Learning Disorders." *Journal of Learning Disabilities* 41, no. 6 (January 1, 2008): 514–23. ERIC (EJ814278), ISBN 0–385–26094–6.

Senge, P., *The Fifth Discipline,* Published by Doubleday Dell Publishing Group, Fifth Avenue, New York, New York. 1990.

Skemp, Richard. "Relational Understanding and Instrumental Understanding." *Arithmetic Teacher* 26, no. 3 (1978): 9–15.

Smith, Margaret and Mary Kay Stein. *5 Practices for Orchestrating Productive Mathematics Discussions.* Reston, VA: National Council of Teachers of Mathematics, Inc., 2011.

Smith, Margaret Schwan., Michael D. Steele, and Mary Lynn. Raith. *Taking Action: Implementing Effective Mathematics Teaching Practices in Grades 6–8*. Reston, VA: National Council of Teachers of Mathematics, 2017.

Sousa, David A. *How the Brain Learns*. Thousand Oaks, CA: Corwin, a Sage Publishing Company, 2017.

Stearns, Linda M., Jim Morgan, Mary Margaret Capraro, and Robert M. Capraro. "A Teacher Observation Instrument for PBL Classroom Instruction." *Journal of STEM Education: Innovations & Research* 13, no. 3 (May/June 2012): 7–16. EBSCO (79468725).

Sternberg, Robert J. "Successful Intelligence: Toward a Broader Model for Teaching and Accountability." *Phi Delta Kappa International: Edge* 1, no. 5 (May/June 2006): 3–18.

Stigler, James W. and James Hiebert. *The Teaching Gap*. New York: Free Press, 2009.

Stout, Judith, Donald Kachur, and Claudia Edwards. *Engaging Teachers in Classroom Walkthroughs*. Cheltenham, Vic.: Hawker Brownlow Education, 2014.

Study Skills Strategies (Part 1): Foundations for Effectively Teaching Study Skills. The Iris Center. https://iris.peabody.vanderbilt.edu/module/ss1/.

Thomas, David C. and Kerr Inkson. *Cultural Intelligence: Living and Working Globally*. 2nd ed. San Francisco, CA: Berrett-Koehler Publishers, 2009.

The UDL Guidelines." UDL: The UDL Guidelines. August 31, 2018. http://udlguidelines.cast.org/ .

TIMSS2015.org, http://timss2015.org/#/?playlistId=0&videoId=0 Analysis of International Comparison of math sat 4th, 8th, and 12th grade levels.

University of Michigan. Teaching Works. http://www.teachingworks.org/work-of-teaching/high-leverage-practices.

Usiskin, Zalman. "What Does It Mean to Understand Some Mathematics?" *Selected Regular Lectures from the 12th International Congress on Mathematical Education*, 2015, 821–41. doi:10.1007/978–3-319–17187–6_46.

Using high-performing collaborative teams for mathematics. (2012). Common Core Mathematics in PLC at Work. Bloomington, IN: Solution Tree Press

Villa, Richard A., Jacqueline S. Thousand, and Ann I. Nevin. *A Guide to Co-teaching: New Lessons and Strategies to Facilitate Student Learning*. Thousand Oaks, CA: Corwin, 2013.

Waber, Deborah P. *Rethinking Learning Disabilities: Understanding Children Who Struggle in School*. New York: Guilford Press, 2010.

Wilkerson, Judy R., and William Steven. Lang. *Assessing Teacher Dispositions: Five Standards-based Steps to Valid Measurement Unsing the DAATS Model*. Thousand Oaks: Corwin, 2007.

Windows of Opportunity: Mathematics for Students with Special Needs, edited by C. A. Thornton and N. S. Bley. Reston, VA: NCTM, National Council of Teachers of Mathematics, 1994.

Witzel, Bradley S., and Mary E. Little. *Teaching Elementary Mathematics to Struggling Learners*. New York: Guilford Press, 2016.

Witzel, Bradley S., Paul J. Riccomini, and Marla L. Herlong. *Building Number Sense through the Common Core*. Thousand Oaks, CA: Corwin Press, a SAGE Company, 2013.

About the Editor

Dr. James Freemyer was a high school mathematics teacher for eight years, a high school principal for seventeen years, chair of a graduate education program for eight years, and currently teaches research statistics and organizational change at Indiana Wesleyan University in a doctoral program in leadership. He received Fulbright and Lilly Scholarships to conduct research in Indiana, California, Ireland, Great Britain, South Korea, and Japan in mathematics education. He is a graduate of the doctoral program at the University of North Carolina at Charlotte.

About the Contributors

Dr. Jill B. Branyon taught high school mathematics for over twenty-five years. Twenty-three of those years were spent in Kenya, East Africa, at a private boarding school. She served as academic dean and principal in the school and worked on numerous committees mentoring young people and served on the board of governors of a local orphanage. She has taught mathematics and mathematics education at North Greenville University for fifteen years and is coordinator of Secondary Mathematics Education as well as working with assessments and reporting for the College of Education. She earned a Doctorate of Education from the University of South Carolina.

Dr. Melinda Eichhorn is an assistant professor in the Education Department at Gordon College. Dr. Eichhorn currently teaches courses on special education assessment, the IEP process, and inclusion, while supervising teacher candidates. Her research interests include math learning disabilities, number sense, transition, early intervention in mathematics, teachers' perceptions of mathematics, and the use of professional development to improve math instruction. She is also a mathematics specialist in the Boston Children's Hospital Learning Disabilities Program.

Maria Marolda has been the Senior Mathematics Specialist in the Learning Disabilities Program of Boston Children's Hospital for over thirty years. The Learning Disabilities Program is part of the neurology department. This affiliation has provided her the framework with which to interpret mathematical performance within the context of broader neuro-cognitive features. Ms. Marolda has served as a consultant to public and independent schools across the country on issues related to mathematics education, including assessments/diagnostics, curriculum and instructional practice. She is the author of several books, journal articles and other publications in mathematics for students and teachers.

Dr. Ellen Boiselle is a specialist in child development, with a particular emphasis on the development of mathematical skills in children. She is Associate Director of the Learning Disabilities Program and a Mathematics Specialist in the Learning Disabilities Program at Boston Children's Hospital. Dr. Boiselle has conducted research on qualitative features of mathematics performance as well as the efficacy of various assessment measures in predicting mathematical success. She serves as consultant to many independent and private schools and has published papers on learning disabilities in mathematics.

Dr. Keith A. Walters was a middle school history teacher for nine years and a university professor for nineteen years. Dr. Walters's teaching responsibilities have included a wide range of courses within the California Baptist University single-subject credential program. His current assignment includes educational psychology as well as curriculum theory and development. Dr. Walters's research focus is in the area of teacher development and growth. He is a graduate of the doctoral program at the University of Southern California.

Dr. Rocky Wallace is a former principal of a Kentucky and U.S. Blue Ribbon School and has written or cowritten ten books that focus on servant leadership being the nonnegotiable in growing more effective and healthy classrooms and school communities. He has helped develop graduate education leadership programs in Kentucky at Morehead State, Asbury University, and now Campbellsville University. He is a graduate of the doctorate in strategic leadership at Regent University.

Dr. Lauren Sager was trained as a high school mathematics teacher before deciding to pursue a PhD in mathematics. She currently teaches mathematics at Saint Anselm College and has recently advised secondary education students and supervised student teachers at Gordon College. Her mathematics education research deals with students' understanding of concepts in precalculus courses. She is a graduate of the doctoral program at the University of New Hampshire.

Dave Klanderman has taught a wide variety of math and math education courses at the college level over the past three decades. Dave is a professor of mathematics education at Calvin University. He has also served as a field supervisor for secondary math student teachers. He is one of four authors of *A Pleasure to Measure: Tasks for Teaching Measurement in the Elementary Grades*. His current research interests including learning trajectories for measurement, extrinsic and intrinsic factors that motivate students to learn mathematics, and links between higher dimensions and the Harry Potter novels by J. K. Rowling. He is a graduate of the doctoral program at Northern Illinois University.

CPSIA information can be obtained
at www.ICGtesting.com
Printed in the USA
FFHW011214201119
56100970-62156FF